GOOD
NEIGHBORHOOD

GOOD
NEIGHBORHOOD

The Challenge of Open Housing

MORRIS MILGRAM

W · W · NORTON & COMPANY

New York   London

To Lorna, Gene, and Betty
and to Pauli Murray and A. Philip Randolph

Books That Live
The Norton imprint on a book means that in the publisher's estimation
it is a book not for a single season but for the years.
W. W. Norton & Company, Inc.

Library of Congress Cataloging in Publication Data

Milgram, Morris.
Good neighborhood.

Includes index.
1. Discrimination in housing—United States.
I. Title.
HD7293.M47   1979   301.54'0973   78-27097
ISBN 0-393-00904-1 pbk.

1 2 3 4 5 6 7 8 9 0

Foreword

by W. Sterling Cary

One of the most frightening realities of American life is the intensified racial separation of American society. The civil rights struggle of the sixties mobilized national support which in 1968 resulted in legislation outlawing racially segregated housing and in the *Jones* v. *Mayer* decision declaring segregation in housing unconstitutional. The religious community played a decisive role in making possible these legislative and judicial victories. But civil rights laws have not desegregated American society. Urban centers are being populated by blacks, Hispanics, and other powerless minorities, while whites are seeking the illusion of sanctuary in suburbia. Urban center and suburbia, however, belong to one metropolitan region. The futures of business and industry, public educational systems, employment, the arts, and political structures in American society are all related to the future of our metropolitan regions. The health of those regions is going to be determined by our ability to rid ourselves of the demons which set race against race, the insane illusion that racial identity is more definitive than membership in a common human family. Nowhere in American society is the worship of race more pronounced than in the residential neighborhood.

Good Neighborhood: The Challenge of Open Housing offers ideas for action for those who would pioneer in liberating American history from the curse of racism. The future is open: we can still shape a tomorrow where humanity is more important than race. It is impossible to build that type of future if our residential neighborhoods remain exclusive ethnic ghettos. In choosing where you live, you are making a faith statement, affirming your membership in the human family or defining your being exclusively in terms of ethnicity. For the human family, integration is not an option, it is a necessity.

Reversing the ghettoization of American residential communities will be possible only if there is dramatic growth in the numbers of whites who

1

intentionally move into integrated neighborhoods. The present reality is that white flight causes integrated neighborhoods to quickly become transitional neighborhoods. Minorities still face the practice of racial steering prevalent among real estate brokers—that is, sending whites to white areas and blacks to black or integrated neighborhoods. Such discriminatory policies must not be permitted to end the search of minority families for decent housing in a white community.

Preface

by Karl E. Taeuber

The achievement of harmonious race relations in the United States is a goal that concerned our founding statesmen and that continues to guide political debate and social policy today. More than thirty years ago Nobel-laureate Gunnar Myrdal wrote of America's ideological quest for equality among people as a powerful force for changing unjust laws and social institutions. In the years since he wrote of this "American dilemma," we have witnessed the collapse of much of the legal structure upholding racial segregation. An extraordinary mass movement effected enormous change in the lives of Americans, white and black. Although improvements in race relations have been dramatic, social change does not take the form of uniform advance toward the mountain's peak. Particularly in residential patterns, rapid improvement in formal conditions—indoor plumbing and central heating—has been accompanied by an increasing scale of racial concentration. The separation of Americans into two societies—chocolate cities and vanilla suburbs, in the words of the popular song—re-establishes and perpetuates dual school systems, differential economic and social opportunities, and explosive racial tension.

Social scientists who as citizens share the dream and want to help society climb the mountain can find much in Morris Milgram's book to provoke their interest and challenge their generalizations. Milgram has for many years been what we may call abstractly a "change agent," but there is nothing abstract about the concrete experiences he sets forth in this account of the real world of housing developers, real estate salesmen, prejudiced politicians, struggling community organizations, and mortgage financiers whose handling of billions of dollars is still affected by outmoded and incorrect myths about race and housing. Milgram describes racially integrated housing developments and communities that have succeeded and others that have failed, and he identifies the specific techniques that lead to success or failure. I should like to indicate how this book has had a crucial influence on the way in which I, as a social scientist

3

long concerned with the study of trends in racial segregation, perceive the prospects for future change.

Most studies of racial residential patterns focus on the situation of the minorities and recount the continuing barriers of prejudice and discrimination that restrict freedom of choice in the housing market. Milgram's experience proves that minority "pioneers" are available; the developer who looks can find plenty of minority families with the money and the desire to purchase or rent attractive housing outside the ghettos. The crucial problem the developer faces is retaining and attracting whites. Here Milgram's practical experience puts a simple demographic equation in a new light.

Demographers know that Americans are a highly mobile people. If we consider a community of, say, blacks and whites, then its long-run racial composition is going to be a net result of blacks moving in and out and whites moving in and out. The tendency among both real estate personnel and social scientists looking at a community where blacks are moving in has been to focus on the whites moving out. What Milgram has discovered, and what my demographic knowledge confirms, is that the real key is whites moving in. Any housing project, any community, experiences out-movement; there will always be vacancies. And there are some white families who are so prejudiced they will move to avoid any neighborly contact with blacks or other minorities. But study after study has showed that the vast majority of whites view themselves as unprejudiced, are aware of the need of black families for housing and of their right to purchase or rent wherever they can afford, and are willing to accept the presence of black neighbors. Milgram has learned how to draw on this group of whites to fill his projects, and he tells how others can do the same.

Social scientists tend to forecast from the recent past into the future. For racial segregation in housing, one of the nation's most severe and persistent problems, I can envisage a new future that represents a sharp change from the recent past. The mass movement of Americans, white and black, from the farms to the cities, and from the small cities to the giant metropolitan centers, has come to a close. High birth rates have declined, especially among black families, and this too will bring a reduction in the demand for new urban housing. During the past three

4

decades our major urban centers experienced rapid increases in black population. These demographic conditions have changed, yet our perceptions of the "normal" operation of the housing market for blacks has not changed.

Similarly, our perceptions of the behavior of whites in the housing market have not adjusted to the fact that mass suburbanization has already occurred and that major social and economic forces are directing new interest at close-in as well as far-out locations. Perhaps most important and least recognized is the fact that the "civil rights generation"—those who reached adulthood in the 1960s and later—are now purchasing their first homes and will soon dominate the market.

The most important lesson that Morris Milgram has to offer these young idealists is that their individual actions in the housing market will determine the future of American race relations. The educational task that Milgram sets is to make this generation aware that their own personal perspectives and aspirations for multi-racial contact for themselves and their children will be thwarted if they simply accept the normal workings of the housing market. But if each family, in pursuit of its own ends, affirmatively seeks to make pro-integration moves, a new, quiet, mass movement will emerge. This unheralded movement can in the space of a generation transform American race relations. This new transformation, by altering the separate social structures that give rise to racial myths in succeeding generations, has the prospect for being more fundamental and long-lasting than the dramatic and visible social movements of the past two decades. This is the deeply American revolution that Morris Milgram is pioneering.

Contents

7

CONTENTS

CONTENTS

Photographs between pages 122 and 123

Introduction

In 1952, after learning the housing business for four years, I went to a Philadelphia real-estate leader for advice on getting started as a private developer of multiracial communities. I was told that no white person would ever voluntarily move next door to blacks. This prophecy proved false. In fact, more than six thousand families chose to live in integrated housing built or purchased with funds of companies I organized, and over eleven thousand individuals and scores of institutions have invested about $25 million (over and above mortgages) to make this possible.

The real-estate leader's advice was hardly unusual at the time. America's segregated housing patterns were conceived under conditions of racial and economic discrimination that had long since become institutionalized; the decay they produce is still used as the rationale for their perpetuation, instead of evidence of their failure.

I may not have reached my decision to pioneer as a private developer of integrated housing had it not been for the noted lawyer and poet Pauli Murray. After repeatedly reading her epic poem, "Dark Testament," to audiences around the country, I finally realized that the following lines about the sons of slave traders told us that the ghetto's purpose is to preserve the unfreedom blacks suffered under slavery:

> Traders still trade in double-talk
> Though they've swapped the selling-block
> For ghetto and gun!

It was then that I resolved to do all I could to end the unwritten law that virtually all new and decent housing was for whites only.

11

INTRODUCTION

It may be pertinent to recall that the rise of ghettos took place in violation of the Civil Rights Act of 1866, which states explicitly that "all citizens of the United States shall have the same rights, in every State and Territory, as is enjoyed by white citizens thereof to inherit, purchase, lease, sell, hold and convey real and personal property." Gradually, however, the rights guaranteed by a number of new laws began to be dismantled. By 1873, the Supreme Court began handing down decisions that opened the way to discriminatory practices, culminating in 1896 in the doctrine of "separate but equal" in the *Plessy* v. *Ferguson* case. From then on, right into the 1940s, southern states adopted hundreds of laws that brought segregation to all areas of life. However, racism was not solely confined to the South. When blacks migrated to the cities in the North, they were held back by similar racial barriers. In the field of housing, these barriers were erected by the nation's real-estate brokers and their professional organizations, who implemented policies that effectively circumscribed the areas where blacks were allowed to live. This legacy is still with us today.

Maintaining the ghetto places a severe and unnecessary tax burden on the entire community, black and white. Crime and vandalism, disease, increased police protection, and public assistance exact a high price. As low-income families gradually fill the inner cities and middle-income whites and minorities move to the suburbs, the tax base of our cities is being eroded, resulting in a downgrading of city school systems and a decline in public services. This, in turn, increases the middle-class exodus to the suburbs and further reduces municipal services. It is an unending, vicious circle that can be broken only by drastic actions designed to halt urban decay and racial isolation.

During the last twenty-five years, the legal foundations of almost all racial segregation in the United States have been swept away in the Supreme Court. During this time, great strides toward racial equality have been made. Blacks have moved into new positions of responsibility in local, state, and federal governments; new employment and training opportunities have been opened up; family incomes have increased; and the door to a closed housing market has been pried open a few inches.

However, with the dismantling of practically all programs that were to deal with the problems of poverty, bad housing, education, and neighborhood stabilization, past and present administrations have turned their backs on completing the task the various Civil Rights Acts were enacted to promote. Grants have been cut and subsidies all but eliminated; agencies that were set up to assist the disadvantaged have been closed down, these closings resulting in a further deterioration of our schools, social services, and available low-cost housing.

A recent report of the United States Commission on Civil Rights concludes that the federal government not only played a dominant role in shaping urban growth and development but has also been "a major factor in the creation of segregated residential neighborhoods . . . [by operating] largely within the system of housing discrimination established long before the Government entered the housing market." The commission further notes that the "Federal Government has been timid in its approach to stimulating lower-income housing production in areas in which whites . . . reside," and thus finds "that the forces promoting discrimination in housing hold powerful, if less than universal, sway."[1] The commission recommends that Congress authorize funds for at least six hundred thousand housing units per year between now and 1978; that the Department of Housing and Urban Development should implement the provisions of the Housing and Community Development Act of 1974, which include, for instance, authorizing funds for low-income housing and homeownership; and that the President should direct the Secretary of HUD and the heads of all Federal Agencies with fair-housing responsibilities to give priority to the enforcement of fair-housing laws.

---

1. United States Commission on Civil Rights, *Twenty Years After Brown: Equal Opportunity in Housing* 1975, pp. 167, 168, 175, 179.

INTRODUCTION

Inflation and recession have further compounded the problems by curtailing the housing industry's ability to provide "a decent home for every American family," the proclaimed goal of the Urban Development Act of 1949. Housing has become a depressed industry. Rehabilitation of existing buildings has been neglected. There is a housing shortage in the suburbs caused by the influx of people and businesses from the cities, while the number of vacant or abandoned buildings in the cities continues to increase. In short, the American housing scene is dominated by a massive reduction and deterioration of its housing stock. Preservation and better management are thus vital to prevent a further erosion of our housing inventory.

It is obvious that private efforts alone cannot get the building industry back on its feet. Additional, comprehensive government programs—federal, state and local—will be needed to stem the tide of urban decay.

Nor can neighborhood decay be halted, except through the elimination of "all forms of racial discrimination in the housing market." According to recent studies, residential separatism is one of the chief causes of neighborhood deterioration.[2] Early-warning systems, such as more frequent population censuses, may be required to keep track of a neighborhood's racial composition.

Absent from most housing deliberations are demands for improved methods of housing management and for affirmative marketing techniques, the tools for maintaining or establishing integrated communities. Equally important are economic incentives in the form of financially advantageous mortgages to whites and minorities for pro-integration housing moves—that is, whites moving to integrated or predominantly black areas and blacks moving to white or integrated areas. Some nonprofit groups have started such programs and are achieving the desired results.

2. W. G. Grigsby and L. Rosenburg. *Urban Housing Policy*. Center for Urban Policy Research—Rutgers University (New York, N.Y.: APS Publications, Inc., 1975), p. 217.

Introduction

The current slump in the housing industry has many causes, and these require an equivalent measure of remedies. To list them all would go beyond the scope of this book, which is based on my experience in the housing industry over the past twenty-four years. I believe the evidence it presents will show that racially and economically integrated housing is the only viable answer to the needs of the housing industry and to those of the housing consumer.

My survey of deliberately planned multiracial communities is not meant to be exhaustive; rather, it indicates the scope and nature of the issues in planning and maintaining integrated housing. One of my purposes has been to examine the problems faced by a developer of affirmatively marketed housing and to focus on business realities as well as on consumer needs. A considerable amount of information was gathered through personal interviews, on-site observation, and mail inquiry. My review of the field concentrates on the situation through 1974 but has been updated in some instances—as far as possible—in accordance with more recent developments and newly available material.

GOOD
NEIGHBORHOOD

1

United States Housing Patterns and the Law

The premise of this book is that racially integrated housing is not only an ideal and therefore morally good, but its creation and maintenance is the most practical way to pursue our national health, both socially and economically. How it can be, and has been, achieved both successfully and profitably is the subject of later chapters; first we shall examine the patterns and trends that have led to the prevailing conditions today.

Nondiscrimination in housing did not become federal policy until 1962, and not until 1968, with the enactment of the Federal Fair Housing Law, did the federal government take on an obligation to attempt *affirmatively* to achieve fair housing. By then, the myths and prejudices that established segregated residential patterns had become all too well entrenched, and their debilitating legacy had become reality to Americans of all incomes.

Resistance to Integration

Consumer Resistance

Consumers' fears concerning property values should have been answered once and for all by Luigi Laurenti's famous *Property Values and Race,* published in 1960. This study of ten thousand real-estate transactions in seven cities showed that more often than

19

not property values went up, not down, when blacks entered the housing market. However, in some instances blockbusting techniques temporarily depressed property values, thus convincing substantial groups in the real-estate industry and elsewhere that housing values go down when blacks arrive. Too many of such groups still do not wish to acknowledge the true state of the situation, although repeated studies have confirmed Laurenti's conclusions.

The idea that there are no stable integrated neighborhoods is as widespread as it is untrue, yet it is expressed at every level of our society. A federal Department of Housing and Urban Development (HUD) official in Atlanta said, for instance, "We know of no stable integrated neighborhoods anywhere in the country." Even the very able Charles Silberman, in *Crisis in Black and White,* indicated that integration was just a way station between all-white and all-black neighborhoods. And an art editor of a New York-based magazine—a person claiming to believe in open housing and integration—when asked if he would seek out an integrated neighborhood, possibly 5 percent black, when moving to the suburbs of New York, declared: "No; a neighborhood that is 5 percent black quickly develops a black majority which, in turn, leads equally quickly to all-black status."

The facts, however, are very different: the number of stable integrated neighborhoods in the United States is growing steadily, as the succeeding chapters will show.

My experience has convinced me that the overwhelming majority of housing consumers are neither actively for nor actively against interracial housing. They simply want the best house at the best price, with the easiest financing.

Probably only 5 or 6 percent of the population would vigorously resist integration and under no circumstances move into an interracial community. But of the growing group of white consumers who recognize an interracial community as an affirmative good, the overwhelming majority make no deliberate attempt to seek out truly multiracial communities when they move. In practice, therefore, the failure to live their principles often leads to the same result as the bigot's refusal to accept integration; such persons simply end up in all-white housing, from which minorities have been barred by lies and threats and stratagems. This failure to make one's preference known plays into the hands of the real-estate industry, which, too often, illegally steers whites to white areas and black to already-integrated or black areas. Unless the white homeseeker makes clear his determination to get housing on a block where blacks already live, and the black homeseeker to get housing in a white area away from the ghettos and on a block which is predominantly white—certainly a more difficult challenge—each will end up with housing that intensifies the residential segregation of minorities.

This brings me to what we may call "Milgram's Law": that the consumer who fails to state his or her determination to seek housing in such a way as to end segregation will nearly always find housing that perpetuates racial separation.

Government Resistance

We shall explore later the provisions of the Federal Fair Housing Act of 1968 along with other current legislation; but legislation is meaningless unless enforcement follows.

Until 1948, when the U.S. Supreme Court ruled racially restrictive covenants in housing unenforceable, reference to race as a criterion for evaluation remained in the underwriting manual of the Federal Housing Administration. A typical reference in the 1936 manual maintains that "the presence of incompatible racial elements results in a lowering of the rating, often to the point of rejection." It was not until July 1954 that FHA Commissioner Norman Mason announced that the government's official policy was to "encourage the development of demonstration open-occupancy projects in suitably located key areas." In January 1956 this policy was restated in a directive to FHA field offices, enjoining their staffs to "continue to take steps to encourage the

21

development of open-occupancy projects in suitable and well-located key areas for both rentals and sales. The positive application of an open-occupancy policy can serve as a helpful example in stimulating private builders and lenders to undertake new open-occupancy developments."[1]

Despite this policy, local FHA officials continued for many years to include on their staffs a considerable number of people whose own social patterns of living made them unreceptive to the idea of open housing. Nonetheless, government officials tend to reflect the social attitudes of their time: as public opinion has steadily moved toward acceptance of an open society, so have the attitudes of some FHA officials.

FHA's old role of opposition to integration has not been fully reversed, by any measure. Essentially, FHA is still part of the establishment concerned with maintaining the status quo in housing. Its pressure for truly multiracial housing is very modest, partly for lack of effort to enforce the law, and partly because FHA officials see their jobs as concerned with a minute portion of the housing field rather than with its overall social aspects. As a result, the U.S. Commission on Civil Rights found that most of the FHA Section 235 housing developments for people of low income were segregated, either almost all-minority or all-white.

George and Eunice Grier recount in their *Privately Developed Interracial Housing* the experience of two interracial communities that were never built.[2] This failure of two well-designed, expertly led, and strongly backed communities is attributed by the authors to FHA's persistent opposition in the 1950s at both local and national levels. Neither development had any difficulties in obtaining a large majority of white applicants.

According to *A Report of the Racial and Ethnic Impact of the*

1. Quoted after Eunice and George Grier, *Privately Developed Interracial Housing* (Berkeley and Los Angeles: University of California Press, 1960), p. 124.

2. *Op. cit.*, Chapter 8, pp. 131–55.

Section 235 Program, issued by the U.S. Commission on Civil Rights in June 1971, "the traditional pattern of separate and unequal housing markets for majority and minority families is being repeated in the operation of Section 235."

The Report also found that much of the new housing in the 235 Program was located in suburban areas and was bought by white families, while most of the existing housing purchased under the Program was located in ghetto areas or changing neighborhoods and was purchased chiefly by minority families. Or, in the words of the Report: "Most of the poor quality housing was existing housing located in the central city and nearly all has been purchased by minority families. Thus, minority families have suffered disproportionately from the abuses that have occurred under the program." Analyzing the anatomy of segregation in 235 housing, the Report asked, "Why has the traditional pattern found in the housing market in general been repeated in the 235 program? A strong arsenal of civil rights laws exists to protect minority home seekers from discrimination in the 235 program as well as in all other housing. Further, the economic rationale for the dual housing market that exists generally has no application here. All eligible families, minority or majority, are required, by statute, to be in the same income range, and all housing, whether suburban or inner-city, whether new or existing, is required, again by statute, to be within the same cost limitations. Nevertheless, the dual housing market persists in the 235 program—a market which is separate and unequal.

"The answer lies in the way in which the program has been administered. Each of the elements involved in the 235 process—real estate brokers, builders, mortgage lenders, interested community groups, Government, and the buyer himself—has played a role in producing the segregated, unequal product."

Discussing the role of FHA, the Report says: "FHA officials, moreover, even though aware of the segregated housing pattern that has developed under the 235 program, have failed to take even minimal steps to change it, despite their legal obligation to

23

do so. FHA and HUD's Office of Equal Opportunity rely mainly on the process of complaints as the mechanism for discovering and eliminating discriminatory practices. The central office in Washington has failed to provide local FHA offices with instructions for affirmative action aimed at broadening the range of housing choice for minority families. Local FHA officials are reluctant to take such action, in some cases, for fear that the central office would not back them up.

"Thus FHA, the agency charged by Congress with responsibility for administering the 235 program, has abdicated its responsibility and, in effect, has delegated it to members of the private housing and home finance industry. In view of the traditional policies and attitudes that have predominated in this industry, the pattern of separate and unequal housing under the 235 program has been inevitable. Until FHA abandons its current passive role and becomes a vigorous champion of the rights of minorities and of lower-income families generally, this pattern is unlikely to change."

The Report's findings showed that:

1. Whites generally get better mortgage rates, higher subsidies, and less crowded housing than minority members under the FHA *laissez-faire* policy;
2. Under the Civil Rights Commission's prodding, HUD began only in 1971 to collect racial data on 235-buyers;
3. The much-publicized shoddiness of construction and profiteering by speculators uncovered by Congressman Patman's House Banking and Currency Committee was not limited to 235 housing but reflected lax local FHA standards for all FHA housing —especially in ghetto areas;
4. Faced with FHA apathy, discrimination by most developers, and a desperate need for low-income housing, local civil-rights groups have come to regard integration as an unattainable luxury, and thus settle for more housing in changing neighborhoods. In other words, as the Commission points out, "resegregation lies ahead."

The report further declared that nearly all brokers interviewed by the Commission were convinced that minorities, particularly low-income families, do not want to move into predominantly

24

white areas. Therefore a great deal of activity for FHA Section 235 housing consisted in trying to sell to minorities in integrated neighborhoods. For example, a white Denver broker told the Commission staff that "the majority of our clients are black and Park Hill [an integrated locality] is our area. We work it strongly."

The Report confirms that "many real estate brokers direct their advertisement toward the racial or ethnic market which they desire to serve." Sometimes, brokers insert the word "anyone" in their advertisements to indicate to the black community that the market is open to all citizens. At other times, the advertisements deliberately seek listings in mixed neighborhoods.

The Report concludes that "members of the private housing and home finance industry have played a key role in the development of the patterns of separate and unequal housing under 235 programs," and recommends that:

1. HUD should establish offices in neighborhoods to advise families on low-rent and Section 235 housing;
2. HUD should organize training programs for community groups that wish to undertake counseling in this field;
3. HUD should make use of the racial and ethnic data it now collects to determine the effect its program is having on ethnic concentration. Whenever HUD finds that housing under its program is intensifying racial and ethnic concentrations, immediate on-site investigation should determine the reasons. Where segregation is found, sanctions should be imposed including the disqualification of discriminatory builders.

Resistance by Builders

A life member of the Board of Directors of the National Association of Home Builders recently estimated that about 99.5 percent of the builders in the country are trying to sell their housing to whites only, and that they will continue to do so as long as the Fair Housing Law fails to be vigorously enforced. Today, even the most forward-looking apartment-house owners and builders—that is, those who have decided to stop turning away the blacks who do apply—generally are unwilling to consider affirmative marketing to make blacks aware that they are really welcome. This means that black occupancy stays at the token .5 to 1 or 2 percent that generally exists in the middle-income housing controlled by these owners.

Even those who deliberately open buildings to blacks in specific locations often maintain all-white buildings in other neighborhoods. In California, for instance, a leading publicly held limited partnership, which controls 1,400 apartments (nine of their ten general partners and virtually the entire investment group are liberal in their social thinking, and several limited partners are black) refrained from pursuing a policy of affirmative marketing to blacks. By 1971, practically all of this firm's buildings in white areas had a black occupancy of no more than 0 to 5 percent, rising in some cases to 10 percent. With the agreement of the realtor, a black associate of mine and I tested one of their buildings in white suburbia to see if discrimination was being practiced against the company's stated policy. No apartment was available for my associate, but when I appeared a few minutes later, suddenly an apartment *was* available. I did not take it, but arranged with my associate to call a couple of hours later to inform them how they could reach him if an apartment became available. They took the information but never contacted him about the apartment which obviously had been available all the time. Afterward, the realtor-owner agreed that this was a clear case of discrimination and promised to take steps to correct it, commenting that our experience had confirmed his suspicion that some of his managers were not obeying company policy.

Similar resistance to obeying stated company policy was found from time to time by me and others involved in property management. It is well known in the housing industry that the greatest resistance to integration and to the observance of the Fair Housing Law occurs on the lowest rung of the industry's hierarchy—on the level of apartment-house superintendents and managers, especially in small buildings. In the process of buying buildings, I have occasionally found superintendents and managers boasting of the measures they used to keep buildings all white.

In November 1970, the Greater Dallas Housing Opportunity Center, Incorporated, did a survey for HUD on the extent of compliance with the Fair Housing Act, which involved ninety-four apartment buildings with more than four units.

Teams of two persons, one white and one black, applied for apartments at close time intervals. The results revealed that about half of the buildings discriminated against members of minority groups in violation of federal laws.

It was the belief of the study group that the 45-percent discrimination rate "must be considered as less than the actual rate for the Dallas area."[3] The group also concluded that almost twice as many managers and owners would have discriminated in some future way—for example, in the handling of credit checks—if the black applicant was serious to the point of proceeding toward the actual rental of an apartment.

In Rochester, New York, interracial teams of testers used by the Urban League met with similar experiences. Sometimes the black tester was told, "Unfortunately, there are no recreational facilities for your children," while the white tester was assured of excellent recreational facilities.

Resistance by Real-Estate Brokers

In 1924 the National Association of Real Estate Boards adopted as part of its code of ethics the following declaration: "A Realtor should never be instrumental in introducing into a neighborhood . . . members of any race or nationality, or any individual whose presence will clearly be detrimental to property values in that neighborhood." Realtors drew up and spread the use of restrictive religious and racial covenants, placing vast distances between the black slums of the ghettos and affluent and lily-white urban and suburban areas. The legacy is still with us today. "Every inter-

3. Greater Dallas Housing Opportunity Center, Inc., *Housing Discrimination in Dallas, Texas: A Survey of Compliance with the Fair Housing Act of 1968* (Washington, D.C.: HUD, November 1970), p. 2.

racial neighborhood that has organized to preserve its new and culturally varied way of life has found the real estate practice of steering minorities into and whites away from their community fundamental to the process of complete racial resegregation."[4]

On a national level, there is a widespread understanding among black and white brokers to preserve the status quo of housing segregation, except in those areas that have been opened up in some way by the entry of one or two black families. Then both black and white brokers often proceed to frighten whites into fleeing. Sometimes they buy houses at modest figures, reselling them at substantial profits. An example of this practice was offered by a black neighbor of mine who lives at Greenbelt Knoll in Philadelphia. Some years ago, a black broker, whom he believed to be a friend of his, offered him a house in Germantown, Philadelphia, for $11,000, ostensibly to get him a good buy. He discovered that the broker was making a great deal more than the commission. He had purchased the house for $7,000 and was using the friendship to make a large profit in a neighborhood where the problem was to find white sales, not black. In St. Louis, a similar trend can be observed: For years the real estate industry has been steering virtually all possible black sales to University City, an integrated suburb, while failing to inform whites about the availability of housing in this very attractive university town.

Brokers, who for years managed to keep blacks out of white neighborhoods, are now, on the pretext of obeying the law, pushing sales to blacks in already integrated neighborhoods, rarely telling them of the availability of housing elsewhere. Similarly, most black brokers make no efforts to secure listings in white areas, thus curtailing the freedom of choice for the black home buyer. In order to break this practice, the white broker who has listings only in white suburbia, selling exclusively to whites because no blacks come to his office, should be asked to do all he can to

4. *Racial Steering: The Dual Housing Market and Multiracial Neighborhoods* (Philadelphia: National Neighbors, June 1973), p. 11.

reach black buyers. Until blacks apply on a broad scale and take legal action to secure housing in white areas, most white brokers will continue to act as if they believe that blacks want to live in "their own" neighborhoods.

Resistance by Lending Institutions

Mortgage bankers have generally claimed that they would not dream of practicing discrimination. "Why should we do so?" they ask. "If we could sell financing for refrigerators to Eskimos, we would be delighted."

In franker moments, the same bankers will admit that some of their customers—top brass of huge savings and loan associations, insurance companies, and others—talk one line, while their lower-echelon staff follow a more discriminatory technique. As one mortgage banker put it to me: "It is not that my customers (banks, insurance companies, and others) offer me *lower* prices for mortgages in interracial areas; they are simply not interested in them."

A major mortgage banker in a southern city, who seemed perfectly willing to handle mortgages on all-black, all-white, or integrated apartment houses, was asked the following question: "If you had funds for just one of two mortgages and were asked to give a mortgage commitment to a developer who never admitted blacks, and a mortgage commitment on a virtually identical building in an equally desirable neighborhood to an open-housing developer, where black occupancy was expected to be 10 or 15 or 20 percent, to which group would you give the mortgage?" Without hesitation, the mortgage banker declared: "I would give it to the builder of all-white housing, because it involves less risk for my investors, and it is my job to protect them." That such an action was based on a self-perpetuating myth, and that it might involve violation of the law, had not occurred to him. He went on to insist that all housing in this southern city was really open to everybody, despite the fact that representatives of the city's Human

Relations Commission had indicated that blacks were being steered to transitional or black areas, and whites to all-white sections, by virtually the entire real-estate industry, black and white.

In another instance, a consortium of banks in a northern city was found to be red-lining certain areas as not available for mortgages to blacks, regardless of the fact that the ostensible purpose of the consortium was to open housing in white areas to minority groups. In actual practice, only specific white neighborhoods, especially those predominantly Jewish, were considered open by the bankers.

Resistance by Investors

Even when investors are personally friendly toward the idea of open housing, their advisors, at best, feel the newness of the concept makes interracial housing extremely risky, and often try to dissuade their investors from supporting such enterprises.

Some of the major investors in housing are not individuals but institutions—trade unions, insurance companies, religious funds, and other nonprofit organizations. When I began my program of developing interracial housing, I approached the Ministers and Missionaries Fund of the Baptist Church, asking if they would take FHA-insured mortgages to enable one of the early integrated communities to get started. They explained that the only mortgages they were taking were conventional mortgages on loft buildings in New York City, and the fact that a government-insured mortgage was far freer of risk did not appeal to them; they were unwilling even to seriously discuss price and terms.

Equally disappointing was the response of a Quaker group, which also invested in conventional, uninsured mortgages, this time in Philadelphia. "We are trustees first, and Quakers second," they said, and declined to consider the offer of FHA-insured mortgages.

Over the years, I have found that the fraternal feelings of a major international labor union also stopped at the color line. When they sold a large building which they had owned for many years in the heart of Washington, D.C., it was just as lily white as when they had bought it, and they gave a second mortgage to the buyer, a group which continued to keep it all white for years, at the most attractively low interest rate of 5 percent. When I approached this union for mortgage money for integrated housing, they always advanced some reason for their funds' being earmarked for other housing ventures.

The following examples from my own experience show how these separate elements of resistance can combine to postpone the development of sensible integrated communities. An early incident was the Deerfield Freedom of Residence Case.

Deerfield, Illinois, a Chicago bedroom community, is a village of 10,500 residents in suburban Lake County. In 1959, the Progress Development Corporation, a subsidiary of Modern Community Developers, a national firm I had founded, bought two separate sites a block apart from each other, on opposite sides of the street, and began building two communities. Two models had almost been completed, and sewer and water had been installed for thirty-nine of the fifty-one lots, when word reached the community that this housing development was to be sold on an integrated basis. The community acted as if a major disaster had struck them. After stopping construction on the model houses under the claim of Building Code violations, they agreed in federal court to stop hampering the construction while the courts ruled on our suit for an injunction to stop interference with our civil rights under the Fourteenth Amendment. More specifically, we claimed a conspiracy existed between the trustees of the village, the Board of the Deerfield Park District, and others. Federal District Judge Joseph Sam Perry dismissed the complaint, holding the conspiracy was unproved. On appeal, the U.S. Court of Appeals held that the District Court had erred in dismissing the action, declaring that "the common law immunity of state legislators for their acts . . .

31

does not extend to local officials charged with administering in a *discriminatory* manner the laws so as to preclude Negroes from moving into an all-white community." However, Judge Perry disqualified himself on the grounds that he was prejudiced, and another judge with a busy calendar was assigned the case. Meanwhile, the state courts took our two sites away for public parks, and in 1963 the U.S. Supreme Court declined to hear an appeal of this condemnation.

The following quotations from a report by the U.S. Commission on Civil Rights, issued in 1961, highlight the problem still further: "In the course of its studies, the Commission has found that the power of the local government has sometimes been actively exerted to prevent equal opportunity in housing rather than to foster it."[5]

The Report goes on to cite four cases that had come to the attention of the Commission, including the Deerfield Case: "All involved affirmative action by local governments—action resulting in the exclusion of minorities who either had already moved into the locality or were about to do so. It is doubtful that these four cases are isolated or unique."

This Report, reprinted widely by the American Freedom of Residence Fund, headed by Eleanor Roosevelt and Bishop James A. Pike and formed to secure freedom of residence in Deerfield, strengthened the efforts which exposed the existence of virtually total suburban exclusion of minorities. The story is well told by Harry and David Rosen in their book on the Deerfield Freedom of Resident Case, *But Not Next Door;* its stirring title puts the problem in a nutshell.

Almost simultaneously with the Deerfield Freedom of Residence Case, a similar battle occured in Downington, Pennslyvania, a suburb of Philadelphia in Chester County, where Chester County Community Developers, Incorporated, was working in conjunc-

---

5. *Civil Rights.* Excerpts from the 1961 United States Commission on Civil Rights Report (Washington, D.C.: U.S. Government Printing Office, 1961), Book 4, p. 132.

tion with Modern Community Developers. They bought a site for eighty-five houses and two park areas about a mile from the center of the town, near the homes of a local member of the city council and the local congressman. The site plan was greeted warmly by local officials until word reached them, through an elderly black who needed housing, that the development would be integrated. At that point, the village officials indicated a preference for lots of about half an acre. When we agreed to go along with that, they demanded lots of closer to one acre. As a result, we went to court to secure our zoning.

The decision was slow in coming, and when it came it was so complex that our counsel, James C. N. Paul, recommended not pressing the legal case any further. Our Board then voted to accept an alternate site which the village indicated would win their approval, a site between an all-white and an all-black area in the center of the town. However, the village failed to improve the black area as promised, and FHA gave such low valuations on our proposed housing that the second site, like the first, had to be sold. This resulted in the investors in Chester County Community Developers receiving about 5 percent plus their initial investment.

These obstacles turned out to be typical in Modern Community Developers' early attempts to create integrated housing. In another case, the authorities demanded much bigger sewer and water lines than they had before they received word of our plans for integration, as well as much more expensive road paving. In still another instance, the ground was suddenly needed for the building of a high school. In the latter case, the ground was sold profitably, because our Board had faced the problem of what do if such an issue arose and had resolved not to fight it.

Enforcing the Law: Obstacles and Solutions

Jones v. *Mayer* was the landmark decision by which the U.S. Supreme Court in 1968 outlawed all discrimination in housing. By now, the story of the Joneses is well known: when they attempted to buy a home, they were refused because of race.

Alfred H. Mayer, the builder in the case, told the press that his major reason for opposing the Joneses was that he felt he could not afford to sell to blacks while his competitors were unwilling to do so. The court held his refusal to be illegal.

The *Jones* v. *Mayer* decision upheld the language of an earlier act of Congress (USC Section 1982) enacted in 1866, which provides that "All citizens of the United States shall have the same right, in every State and Territory, as is enjoyed by white citizens thereof to inherit, purchase, lease, sell, hold, and convey real and personal property." Cases brought into court under this decision have been awarded substantial damages.

In ruling that Mayer's refusal was illegal, the Court declared that: "when racial discrimination herds men into ghettos and makes their ability to buy property turn on the color of their skin . . . it . . . is a relic of slavery. At the very least, the freedom that Congress is empowered to secure under the Thirteenth Amendment includes the freedom to buy whatever a white man can buy, the right to live where a white man can live. If the Congress cannot say that being a free man means at least this much then the Thirteenth Amendment made a promise the Nation cannot keep" (U.S. Supreme Court, *Jones* v. *Mayer,* June 1968).

Shortly after the decision, Samuel H. Liberman, the attorney who had argued the Jones case successfully before the court, joined me in summarizing[6] the reasons we thought the *Jones* v. *Mayer* decision would prove more effective in eliminating discrimination in housing than past legislation had been. Subsequent events have supported our analysis:

1. The law applied in this case applies to all segments of the housing market and cannot be criticized as leaving any one group at a competitive disadvantage.

6. "The Supreme Court Decision on Open Housing: What it Means to Apartment Builders," *Compendium of Multifamily Housing,* vol. III, (Washington, D.C.: National Association of Home Builders, 1968).

2. It applies to owners as well as agents, thus taking brokers, managers, and other intermediate parties off the spot. These people simply have to comply with the law now. They cannot be criticized for it by neighboring tenants or owners.
3. The availability of immediate injunctive relief discourages procrastination or delay by owners or managers.
4. The breadth of the coverage indicates that there is no place where whites can flee into restrictive living, for the simple reason that exclusion is no longer possible anywhere. The realization of this fact should tend to reassure white property owners and prevent the kind of panic selling which, in some instances, has resulted in the past in the resegregation of all-white areas into all-black areas.

Beginning on January 1, 1969, the Federal Fair Housing Law of 1968 made it unlawful for an owner, manager, or any other person to refuse to rent an apartment to anyone because of race, color, religion or national origin, or to discriminate by limiting rentals or length of a lease under which an apartment can be rented. Single-family houses were covered by law as of January 1, 1970, unless sold directly by the owner without use of a real-estate broker. However, the *Jones* v. *Mayer* decision extended the law to all housing, so that even single-family houses sold directly by the owner can no longer be sold in a discriminatory fashion.

Enforcement of the law, depending on the factors involved, can be won: (1) by HUD on complaint of an aggrieved minority person; (2) by a state or local human rights agency if the area has a state or local law comparable to the Federal Fair Housing Law; (3) by court action brought by the aggrieved minority person; (4) by the U.S. attorney general, if he feels that the person or company selling or renting is engaged in a pattern or practice of resistance to the full enjoyment of equal opportunities in housing. It is estimated that about 55 million dwelling units are covered by the Federal Fair Housing Law, also known as Title VIII of the Civil Rights Act of 1968. However, only 1,028 complaints were made to HUD under this law in 1970. Two years later, the processing of complaints had not appreciably increased: Of the 1,474 complaints handled by HUD directly, 238 were still pending by the end of fiscal 1972, while 1,057 complaints were referred to state and local fair-housing agencies which, during the same period, completed no more than 164 of these cases.[7]

By August 1971, the Housing Section of the U.S. Department of Justice, Civil Rights Division, headed by Frank Schwelb and his staff of nineteen attorneys and six full-time research analysts, had filed 100 cases under Title VIII.

At the time the Housing Section was formed in October 1969, the Civil Rights Division had filed fourteen cases under Title VIII, had participated as *amicus curiae* in six other fair-housing suits, and had intervened in one other case.[8] In the first ten months following its formation, the Housing Section filed thirty-eight additional cases. By August 1970, twenty-one cases had been successfully completed: twenty cases were "by consent" decrees, which usually included affirmative relief as well as a prohibition against discrimination, and one case was settled by court decision. The Section also attempted to bring a variety of Title VIII action suits to obtain rulings on as many provisions of the law as possible, although they were somewhat limited by the nature of the complaints that were received.

In response to the rising number of cases filed and brought to trial, and the need to maintain its pace, the Housing Section expanded its staff in 1974 to 24 attorneys and 8 research analysts, who, during the first three months of the year, had filed ten cases, intervened in one suit, and filed Motions for Supplemental Relief in three actions, one of which included a civil-contempt motion. Since its inception in 1969, the section has filed 177 cases and 7 motions for Supplemental Relief.

Typical of the consent orders the Housing Section has secured is the case of the XYZ Realty Company[9] in Illinois. The com-

7. *Equal Opportunity in Suburbia.* A Report of The United States Commission on Civil Rights. (Washington, D.C.: July 1974), p. 42.
8. These and the following statistics have been obtained from the Civil Rights Division of the United States Department of Justice.
9. Not its real name.

plaint alleged that the broker had refused to show black persons houses for sale in white neighborhoods, while making such listings available to whites. XYZ Realty denied this. Following the presentation of the evidence at the trial, the government and XYZ Realty agreed on the entering of an order which permanently enjoined XYZ Realty, or its owners, officers, agents, employees, or successors from:

1. Making unavailable or denying any dwelling to any person because of race or color.

2. Discriminating against any person in the terms, conditions, or privileges of sale of a dwelling, or in the provision of services . . . relating to the financing of such dwelling, because of race or color.

3. Refusing or failing to show or sell homes to any person because of the race or color of persons occupying dwellings in the neighborhood of such homes.

4. Making, printing, or publishing, or causing to be made, printed or published, any notice, statement or advertisement, with respect to the sale of a dwelling that indicates any preference, limitation or discrimination based on race or color, or an intention to make such preference, limitation, or discrimination, with the exception of the affirmative action required of the defendant by paragraph (3.) (b.) below.

5. Representing to any person, because of race or color, that any dwelling is not available for inspection or sale when such dwelling is in fact available."[10]

The consent decree further ordered XYZ Realty to adopt and implement an affirmative program in compliance with the Fair Housing Act.

in order to insure that in the future all dwellings listed and shown by the defendant in all areas in which it does business will be made available for inspection by and sale to black persons on the same basis that they are made available for inspection by and sale to white persons. Such an affirmative program shall include, but shall not be limited to, the following steps:

10. This and the following excerpts are quoted by permission of Judge William J. Bauer, United States District Court for the Northern District of Illinois.

GOOD NEIGHBORHOOD

(1.) The defendant shall, within 30 days of the entry of this order, conduct an educational program for its sales personnel and other agents and employees to inform them of the provisions of this decree and their duties under the Fair Housing Act. Such program shall include the following:

(a.) A copy of this decree shall be furnished to each agent and employee.

(b.) By general meeting or individual conference, the owners of XYZ Realty, Inc., shall inform each agent and employee of the provisions of this decree and of the duties of the company and its agents and employees under the Fair Housing Act. Each agent and employee shall also be informed that his failure to comply with the provisions of this decree shall subject him to dismissal or other disciplinary actions by XYZ Realty.

(c.) Each agent and employee shall sign a statement that he has read this decree and received the instructions described in the preceding paragraph.

(2.) The defendant shall inform the public generally and its customers or clients specifically of the defendant's nondiscriminatory policy by the following action:

(a.) Each of the defendant's listing contracts, exclusive or non-exclusive, shall contain the printed statement, in conspicuous type size at least as large as that used herein, that "homes and other dwellings will be shown and made available for sale to all persons without regard to race or color in compliance with the 1968 Fair Housing Act, 42 U.S.C. 3604." In addition, at the time of listing, sellers are to be orally informed of this provision.

(b.) The defendant shall post and maintain a sign, of conspicuous size and in a conspicuous location, in each of its offices, containing the language set forth in the preceding paragraph.

(c.) The defendant shall periodically (at least once per month for the first two years following the entry of this Order and once per quarter thereafter) place conspicuous advertisements in public media which are directed primarily at a black audience, . . . stating that XYZ Realty, Inc., has listings of homes available for inspection and sale throughout the . . . locality in which the company has such listings.

(d.) In all its advertising, the defendant shall avoid the use of words or phrases which indicate, by common usage or understanding, a preference that the homes advertised be shown or sold to persons of a particular race or color.

(e.) Current listings of the defendant are to be made available by locality but not by address, to all interested civic groups, upon request.

(3.) The Defendant shall develop and implement procedures to insure that all black prospective purchasers are provided with an informed choice of homes for inspection and sale throughout the localities in which the company has listings, including, but not limited, to the following:

(a.) XYZ Realty shall adopt a uniform procedure for informing all prospective purchasers of the financial requirements necessary or desirable for the purchase of a home, including the amount of family income and down payment required and the sources of mortgage loans for home purchases.

(b.) The defendant shall instruct each of its agents and employees that when a black prospective purchaser inquires either with respect to a specific home listed with XYZ Realty and located in or near an area known by the company or its personnel to be a predominantly black or rapidly integrating area or (2) with respect to homes in or near such an area generally, the prospective purchaser is to be informed of homes in his price range, if any exist, listed by XYZ Realty and located outside such areas. However, after being so informed, no prospective purchaser is to be denied the opportunity to inspect or buy such homes inquired about.

(4.) The defendant shall recruit and hire black agents and employees on the same basis as white agents and employees are recruited and hired. Black agents and employees hired by the defendant prior to the entry of this decree and black agents and employees hereafter hired by the defendant shall be assigned duties and responsibilities, including those involving the general public, without regard to race or color and on the same basis as white agents and employees are assigned.

The Court further ordered that ninety days after this decree, at three-month intervals for four years, XYZ should file with the court and with the attorney for the plaintiff a report listing every home, including address, price, and available financing, the number of white prospects who inquired in person about the home, the number of shown homes and the date, firm commitment and address and price of each home sold to whites. For each nonwhite prospect who inquired, the report should list name; race and address;

dates of contact and locality where contact was made; who served the prospect; type of home desired, size, and price; income of prospect and cash available; if possible, financing he could carry; and whether the prospect requests a specific home or a specific area.

The order also required XYZ Realty to supply the address of each home recommended and shown to minorities, the reasons for rejection of each home, the address and price of the home purchased by the prospect, and the kind of financing secured for the purchase.

In addition, the Court demanded the names and addresses of those sellers who, mindful of their duty to show all citizens regardless of race, had refused to give XYZ Realty exclusive listings. XYZ Realty was also enjoined to furnish the name of the real-estate company which subsequently received the exclusive listing; the names of financial institutions which refused mortgages to nonwhite buyers seeking to purchase in white areas; and the names of buyers as well as the reasons for the refusal of financial assistance. Furthermore, the Court asked for copies of all real-estate advertisements placed by XYZ Realty and a listing of name, race, date of employment, and office assignment of each sales agent hired by the XYZ Realty Company. XYZ was also ordered, forty-five days after the decree, to file with the Court and the government a report detailing the preliminary steps taken to implement the decree. This report was to include copies of the various forms used for listings and was to indicate whether training sessions on the decree and its implementation were carried out for all employees. In the view of the Court, the keeping of racial records in order to comply with the decree would not be considered discriminatory. At the same time, the defendants were assured by the Court that reports provided under the decree would be treated confidentially. The decree, ordered on February 25, 1971, was signed by Judge Julius J. Hoffman of the United States District Court with consents from representatives of XYZ Realty and the U.S. Department of Justice.

A very good summary of the enforcement of the Federal Fair Housing Law of 1968 is contained in the Report of the United States Commission on Civil Rights, *Equal Opportunity in Suburbia* (July 1974). As we have mentioned earlier, an astonishingly small number of complaints are handled under this law. Surveying the scene, the commission concluded that "the zeal with which the Federal officials carried out policies of racial discrimination in the early days of Federal involvement has not been matched [so far] by a similar enthusiasm for implementing equal housing opportunity." This is due, in part at least, to the gross understaffing of the division responsible for the enforcement of the law at both the Justice Department and HUD.

The Nixon Administration's statement of June 1971 strongly opposed racial discrimination in housing, while refusing to back economic integration. The statement, nevertheless, gave an important tool to federal officials who want to act vigorously in support of open housing. Thus in August 1971, the Washington Center for Metropolitan Studies received a HUD Urban Renewal Demonstration Grant of $175,000 to develop new techniques for the opening up of Washington's suburbs. Besides making black families aware of available housing and enabling them to contact brokers, make applications, and, if denied housing, file complaints, this project also aimed at familiarizing both black and white homeseekers with the existence of the Fair Housing Act. The research conducted by the Center resulted in a set of consumer-information documents, *Homeseekers' Guides,* to a number of major suburbs of metropolitan Washington, in addition to a special comprehensive guide to low- and moderate-cost apartments in the same areas. By providing minority families with equal access to information on the housing market, the Guides have substantially contributed to the breaking down of the information monopoly, that is, the "special" listing services of the real-estate industry. Each guide covers a major suburban area and consists of the county's map, listing relevant housing information (location, price, lot size, architecture, age, and distance from Washington) in an easily usable format at reasonable prices ($1.00 to $1.50). Recipients of the Guides include, among others, government agencies; federal, local and state officials, and legislators; and military installations, housing organizations, and labor unions. A considerable number of Guides were distributed free of charge to blacks and black-oriented organizations. As the Guides also attempt to educate home-seekers on the nature and implication of the Federal Fair Housing Act and its guarantee of equal access to the housing market, they should furnish a useful tool for enforcing fair-housing laws.

Thirty American states, including one in the South (Kentucky), have passed fair-housing legislation. According to the 1970 Census, 63 percent of the population, that is, 129 million people, live in these thirty states.

In addition, 345 cities and counties, including two in the South (Alexandria and Arlington, Virginia) have enacted nondiscrimination housing ordinances; 114 of these ordinances are in states with no equal-housing legislation.

If one adds the population of these areas to the thirty states that have enacted fair-housing legislation, the percentage of Americans living in areas which support equal housing for all citizens rises to 75 percent.

According to HUD's General Counsel, twenty-four of the thirty state laws are now "generally equivalent" to federal standards. Several additional state laws are under review.

But enactment of laws is almost meaningless unless enforcement follows.

The Nixon Administration's promise to "fully discharge its own particular responsibilities" was, as we now know, broken: housing, in particular the production of low-cost housing, was drastically curtailed by the same administration's callous cuts of vital subsidies. By 1976, they had yet to be restored.

The long-term, downhill trend toward the decay of our central cities will not be reversed until an American president, prodded by sensible action by the housing industry and housing consumers to promote economic as well as racial integration, launches vigorous efforts for economically integrated housing, along the lines pioneered by Irving J. Fain at University Heights, Providence, Rhode Island.

Housing and Planning Programs as Instruments for Enforcing the Law

The Shaker Communities Housing Office

What may be the most important change in the field of housing in the decade of the 1960s took place quietly in Shaker Heights, a suburb of Cleveland, Ohio. Here, the recognition that educational segregation is an outgrowth of the uniracial character of a neighborhood's housing pattern persuaded the local school board to support the Shaker Communities Housing Office in its efforts to promote the development of integrated communities.

Since 1967, the City of Shaker Heights and the Board of Education have been jointly financing the Shaker Communities Housing Office. The Office employs one full-time and fourteen part-time staffers, who maintain a complete roster of homes and apartments for sale and rent and, without fee, bring buyers and sellers together with the cooperation of area real-estate brokers, homeowners, and community associations.

Cooperating with the Shaker Communities Housing Office is the Shaker Communities Development Foundation, headed by William B. Hammer and supported by contributions from citizens and foundations. In 1971, the Foundation owned five housing units and ten second mortgages. Its functions are focused on the Moreland Elementary School in order to help maintain an interracial community.

Basically, the Foundation assists with secondary financing and acquires distress properties whenever possible, putting them into shape for rental or sale within the Shaker housing program. The

Shaker Communities Housing Office is a pioneering venture. Here, for the first time in the United States, a local government and a local board of education use public funds to strengthen housing integration by aiding house-hunters. We shall describe later in more detail the effectiveness of this program, and how it works.

The Miami Valley Regional Plan

The Miami Valley region in southwestern Ohio is a five-county area which includes the city of Dayton in Montgomery County. The population of this region numbers about 900,000, of whom 11 percent are black. Between 1960 and 1970, the overall population of urbanized Montgomery County increased. During the same period, Dayton's total population declined, while that of its black residents rose by 30 percent. Simultaneously, the average price of a house in the Dayton area rose from $17,500 in 1966 to $25,300 in 1969, while vacancies dropped to 1.6 percent. This situation created a serious housing shortage, in particular among the 55,000 households of Montgomery County whose annual income is less than $7,000.

One of the agencies charged with remedying this situation is the Miami Valley Regional Planning Commission (MVRPC), which was created in 1964 to conduct comprehensive planning activities in an area covering five member counties and thirty-seven member municipalities. In 1969, after the Department of Housing and Urban Development had added the planning of housing to the responsibilities of planning agencies funded by it, MVRPC initiated its Housing Program. This coincided with the first black moves into suburban areas, alarming some local mayors, who turned to MVRPC for advice.

The chief purpose of the Commission's Housing Program was to assess the area's housing needs and offer ways of solving the problems. The most critical housing needs involved, of course, the low- and moderate-income groups, that is, those who are unable to compete for decent housing in the open market. In the Miami

44

Valley Region—as elsewhere—the available low-cost housing is not only in short supply, but is mostly concentrated in areas of physical, social, and economic deterioration.

The Miami Valley Regional Planning Commission has produced a number of valuable studies, in particular, the *Plan for the Miami Valley Region*—also known as the Dayton Plan—which contains one of the basic concepts of the program: the planned expansion of geographic housing opportunities, or scatterization. The importance of the plan lies in its function as a framework for efforts that will increase the lower-income housing supply as well as the range of geographic choices for low-income households. Soon after its publication, the plan was unanimously endorsed in September 1970, by thirty-seven local elected officials who serve as commissioners on the forty-two-member MVRPC.

Using the 1970 Census figures, the Commission established that the Miami Valley Region had a "total housing deficit of some 20,000 dwelling units, of which about 14,000 were needed for low and moderate income households."[11] To reduce this deficit during the next four years, the Dayton Plan recommended the dispersal of 14,000 federally subsidized housing units throughout the Dayton metropolitan area on a "fair share" basis, giving due consideration to questions of community needs and community absorption capacities. Translated into practical terms, this means the building of low-cost housing throughout Dayton's surrounding suburbs—most of them all white. The fair-share program not only contributes toward the breaking up of large concentrations usually associated with public housing, but was also designed to relieve the pressures of urban growth by broadening the geographic choices of low- and moderate-income families. In addition, by limiting and controlling the momentum of outward minority expansion, the plan should help to reduce both white and black middle-class resistance to the implementation of the Fair Share Housing Plan.

11. MVRPC, *Housing for the Miami Valley Region: A Regional Plan and Program.* (Dayton, Ohio: MVRPC, April 1974), p. 11.

Resistance to the plan was, of course, to be anticipated. Thus members of the Miami Valley Regional Planning Commission have spent much time describing, explaining, and defending the plan at local meetings. Support of the plan has come from an unexpected quarter: the business elite of Dayton. Governed by a city manager and a council, Dayton lacks a strong political force. "When action is required, it is the newspapers and the business elite that call the tune. The two work in tandem. Jim Fain, editor of *The Daily News,* one of the two newspapers here, and a leading advocate of dispersal, is . . . chairman of the Area Progress Council (APC), a select group of business leaders created in the early 1960s to give form to its management of community affairs."[12] In the aftermath of the 1966/67 riots in West Dayton's black ghetto, the APC accorded low- and moderate-income housing top priority. The Fair Share Housing Plan was even informally cleared with the APC, and Jim Fain, through his newspaper, joined the Miami Valley Regional Planning Commission in the task of informing local officials, the public, and leaders of metropolitan Dayton society of the plan's goals and provisions. In addition, the Chamber of Commerce pledged $50,000 as seed money for subsidized housing, and the Junior League, consisting chiefly of wives and daughters of APC members, also extended seed money and support for scatterization as a means of opening up suburbia. Although acceptance of the plan and acceptance of subsidized housing in the suburbs are two entirely different problems, the business elite's support seems unrelenting. "Without the support of the business community and the newspapers," Dale Bertsch, Executive Director of MVRPC, declared, "we would have published a technical dissertation that would not have been carried out in action." Nevertheless, barriers in the way of implementing the Dayton Plan do exist, ranging from anticipated objections by some whites to having black neighbors, to institutional obstacles, such as zoning ordinances. As far as the latter is concerned, staff members of MVRPC have col-

12. *Wall Street Journal,* May 11, 1972. Also for the following.

lected and reviewed all such ordinances in order to identify those provisions that impede the production of low-cost housing within the region. In addition, they monitor housing advertisements to ascertain whether the ads meet the standards of FHA affirmative marketing requirements, and they participate in the development of an "area-wide affirmative marketing plan along with the Dayton Urban League and the Dayton Area Human Relations Council."[13]

What tools are available to the Miami Valley Regional Planning Commission for enforcing the Federal Fair Housing Law? To begin with, there are the 1964 and 1968 Civil Rights Acts, but there is also the A-95 review process, an intergovernmental device set up by the Federal Office of Management and the Budget to insure compliance with federal legislation. The Miami Valley Regional Planning Commission "as the areawide review agency, is responsible for this review."[14] This process ensures that federal programs will not duplicate regional or local efforts. Developments with more than fifty single-family units or one hundred multifamily units are subject to review by the MVRPC. Since 1969, the Miami Valley Regional Planning Commission has used the review process for evaluating new assisted housing in the area under its jurisdiction, for discouraging low- and moderate-income housing in areas that have reached, or are about to reach, their numerical targets, and for generally insuring compliance with the Civil Rights Acts. The A-95 review process has proved a useful means for encouraging the concept of scatterization in areas until recently closed to subsidized housing. On the other hand, MVRPC was able to prevent construction of a 456-unit subsidized housing development in Madison Township as being directly in the path of black expansion from neighboring West Dayton, and therefore likely to turn into a ghetto before long.

From 1971 to 1974, sixteen times more new housing for low- and moderate-income families has been built in the Miami Valley

---

13. MVRPC, *op. cit.,* p. 7.
14. *Ibid.,* p. 22.

Region than in any previous year. This includes all types of housing, from single-family homes to high-rise apartments for the elderly and handicapped. Changes can be observed in the pattern of geographic location of lower-income housing, for most of it has been dispersed over a wide area, rather than being concentrated in center-city locations. Concurrently with this development there is a growing awareness of the region's housing problems among its people.

By January 1973, the regional housing deficit had declined from 20,000 dwelling units to 18,000 units, while the deficit for low-cost housing had decreased from about 14,000 units to 12,400 units. Prior to January 1970, the Miami Valley Region had about 3,296 assisted housing units, of which 95 percent were located in the city of Dayton. "Since January 1970, 3,744 assisted housing units have been built, acquired or are under construction, with 50 percent in Dayton and 50 percent in suburban or outlying areas. In addition, 2,510 more units are in the proposal stage, with 27 percent in Dayton and 73 percent in other areas. These figures include public housing, Section 236 rental housing and rent supplement units."[15] These figures do not include the 733 completed rehabilitation units, nor Section 235 or Farmers Home Administration Section 502 single-family homes for moderate-income groups, almost all in outlying or suburban areas.

Two significant changes are reflected in the MVRPC experience. First, there is the marked increase in the provision of low- and moderate-income housing in the Miami Valley Region, which represents an annual increase in the rate of production of roughly 1,600 percent. Today, some twenty-five thousand persons live in about 8,500 assisted housing units.

The second and equally important change occured in the geographic distribution of lower-income housing. In 1970, no more than 5 percent of subsidized housing had been located outside

15. MVRPC, *Housing for the Miami Valley Region: The Search for a Decent Home.* (Dayton, Ohio: MVRPC, March 1973), p. 9.

Dayton city. Three years later, some 75 percent of the proposed or finished housing for low- and moderate-income groups was in suburban or outlying districts.

Despite these gains, the Region's inventory of low-cost housing remains short of some 12,360 dwelling units. Because of the Housing Program's emphasis on low- and moderate-income housing, the lower-income housing supply was increased by 4 percent, at a time when lower-income households in the Region increased by only 2.7 percent.

The Fair Share Housing Plan—in spite of its modest gains—has engendered a great deal of national attention, largely because MVRPC managed to enlist the support of local elected officials in their campaign to open the suburbs to subsidized housing, an undertaking which still arouses resistance and fierce partisan debates. But Jim Fain, the editor of *The Daily News,* questions the efficacy of education alone in the attempt to reduce people's long-held prejudices. He argues that "bold political muscle is needed" . . . to open "Dixie suburbs." Nobody expects, of course, that a large number of inner-city blacks will rush into suburbia. C. J. McLin, a black state representative from Dayton, thinks that relatively few black families will move into the suburbs as long as the general atmosphere remains unfriendly. But the fact that blacks can move to the suburbs will give them, in the words of McLin, at least "the right to refuse to live there, instead of the community refusing to let them live there. And that's significant for black people."[16]

The Social Security Administration's Housing Program

Some federal agencies, including the Department of Defense, the Social Security Administration, and the State Department, have developed housing programs to aid their personnel. A good example is the program of the Social Security Administration, which provides a kit called "So You're Moving to Baltimore," for per-

16. *Wall Street Journal, op. cit.*

sonnel moving into its huge Baltimore headquarters complex. Commenting on the kit and the Baltimore complex, *Neighbors*[17] declared: "It is one aspect of an aggressive effort by the Social Security Administration's Housing Service to assist its employees to find housing and to make sure all of the Baltimore area is open to all Social Security Administration employees. Since 1970, the Housing Service has helped more than 10,000 government employees with their housing problems, 57 percent of them black, and is the only federal agency, except for appraising services, to be a member of a multiple listing service."[18]

When the Social Security Administration realized that it could not attract enough high-level minority employees because of the lack of open housing, the agency set up its own Housing Service. They hired a housing officer, Ronald Blavatt, who developed a program that provides housing referrals, educational programs, cooperation with other organizations, and assistance for employees encountering discrimination. Members of Mr. Blavatt's staff help employees to find homes or apartments to rent or buy, deal with grievances against landlords, and advise on price ranges, taxes, leases, financing, and community facilities. Special efforts are made to assist employees who seek housing in multiracial neighborhoods. In 1973, the Housing Service distributed 125,000 copies of their "Fair Housing and You" pamphlet through the Baltimore County public school system to educate residents of Baltimore County, which is 96 percent white, on fair-housing problems.

Since the full-time staff of the Housing Service is small, it relies on the part-time services of two hundred volunteers drawn from employees working at SSA headquarters. These volunteers are trained to provide help in emergency situations such as floods, evictions, and deteriorating properties. They also give information on fair-housing laws, conduct tours to new developments in the

17. The news letter of National Neighbors, a federation of multiracial neighborhood organizations.
18. November–December, 1970.

Baltimore metropolitan area, and even put on a play, *For Sale,* by Joan Vail Thorne, for several organizations in the community and the Greater Baltimore Board of Realtors. In addition, there is a Legal Services Panel consisting of fifty SSA attorneys who extend free legal counseling on housing to employees.

In order to reach a wider public, the Housing Service conducted seminars on fair housing. The first, entitled "Equal Housing Opportunities, 1971" was televised for over two hours of prime evening time, with a live audience of five hundred persons in attendance. This seminar, the first of its kind in the country, brought together interests and experts involved in housing to discuss equal-housing opportunities and the implementation of such policies. The program was sponsored by the Social Security Administration and seven other groups from business and industry. Shortly after the seminar, Maryland passed its Fair Housing Law, and the first black person was appointed to the state's Real Estate Commission.

A second seminar, "Residential Mortgage Problems in Metropolitan Baltimore," was presented in June 1972. This time, the seminar was co-sponsored by over fifty major employers; their sponsorship represented a significant change in their thinking, which until then had not included their own involvement in their employees' housing problems.

In September 1973, the SSA Housing Service became a HUD 237 counseling agency. Under this agreement, the Social Security Administration provides counseling services for its employees who have been turned down for an FHA mortgage because of poor credit ratings. Once the SSA determines that an employee has received sufficient counseling to be a good candidate for an FHA-insured mortgage, it can recommend to HUD that the employee's house be insured.

The Housing Service also cooperates with the Maryland State Real Estate Commission, the Citizens Planning and Housing Association, Baltimore Neighborhoods, Inc., the Baltimore County Community Relations Committee, the Regional Planning Council, and the Governor's Landlord-Tenant Commission.

One shortcoming of the emphasis of many excellent programs of government agencies in this field is that helping minorities to secure housing takes up most of their time. Almost no educational effort is aimed at encouraging white government employees, especially in major metropolitan areas, to recognize the significance of their housing moves. However, closed housing in suburbia not only violates the rights of minorities to live where they wish, but it also forces our major cities into a heavily black status. Most white government employees who move—even liberals who work for civil-rights agencies—tend to gravitate toward white suburbia, from which blacks are *de facto* barred by the racial steering practiced by the housing industry. Government agencies have not yet begun to resolve this challenge, although the enforcement of the Federal Fair Housing Act of 1968 provides at least part of the solution.

Another shortcoming associated with the efforts of governmental agencies is that the effects of their housing programs can be overbalanced by the effects of other agencies' values and activities. For instance, faced with a choice between convenience and ensuring adequate housing for its minority employees, the Social Security Administration, despite its excellent housing program, chose organizational convenience. The proposed expansion of its headquarters in Baltimore County, Maryland, illustrates this point. Pursuant to a Memorandum of Understanding with the General Services Administration that HUD would determine the availability of low- and moderate-income housing on a nondiscriminatory basis in locations proposed for federally constructed buildings, HUD found the site for the projected expansion inappropriate because Baltimore County lacked adequate housing for SSA's minority employees. SSA, however, took the position that the proximity of its headquarters to the City of Baltimore, with a sufficient supply of minority housing, made the lack of it in Baltimore County irrelevant. After intense community and political pressures were brought against the proposed expansion in Baltimore County— mainly for reasons unrelated to minority housing—SSA agreed to locate the minor part of the planned expansion in downtown Baltimore and the major one near its headquarters in Baltimore County.

Despite the commendable efforts of its employee housing programs, the federal government has failed to educate both its white and black employees on the social consequences of their housing moves. This laxity, along with the government's concomitant unwillingness to be inconvenienced by the implications of its building activities, continues to nourish the increasing segregation in Washington, Baltimore, and other cities with substantial federal payrolls.

2

Privately Developed Multiracial Housing: A Survey

Early Enterprises

Housing is everybody's problem. Our homes are more than mere commodities for sale or rent. Where we live forms part of our identity. The quality of housing and its free availability thus determine not only the behavior of people but also the condition of a neighborhood. Yet the existence of slums, and of ghettos in particular, contradicts some of the basic tenets our society was founded to uphold, such as free choice and equality of opportunity. The evident gap between our ideals and reality, between promises and performance, induced me to become a developer of integrated housing.

My late father-in-law, the engineer and builder William M. Smelo, repeatedly asked me to join his firm. When I recognized the opportunity for social change involved in the development of housing, I told him I would do so, provided I could build houses for *all* people. We shook hands on an agreement that his firm would back me financially in my efforts to develop integrated housing, if I would learn the business. This I did, beginning in June 1947. For four and a half years I thus built houses for whites only while my conscience hurt.

In 1952, I announced my determination to retool to open-occupancy housing at a meeting at the home of Frank Loescher, then Director of the Mayor's Commission on Human Relations in Philadelphia. I burned my bridges behind me and told the group that I would rather be a laborer and live in a slum than build housing for whites only; that I would, in fact, build nothing, not even commercial properties, until I could get my open-occupancy housing projects under way.

For seventeen long months the search went on to find investors willing to put their funds alongside our firm's money. The first person to agree was a builder, George E. Otto, then co-chairman of the Philadelphia Friends Social Order Committee. However, I refused to set up the corporation without black investors, since, in my view, integrated housing should not be built with an all-white investing group. We got under way when the late Dr. William H. Gray, Jr., former president of Florida A & M College and pastor of the Bright Hope Baptist Church, joined us. With him came his friend the late Dr. Nathaniel S. Duff, a Tuskegee graduate and physician, and superintendent for decades of the Sunday school of his church. Our board of directors as finally organized consisted of six whites and three blacks: Dr. Duff, Dr. Gray, and Dr. E. G. McGruder of Bristol, Pennsylvania, a physician with a largely white practice.

We bought the fifty-acre Concord Park tract in Trevose, Bucks County, Pennsylvania, for $100,000, and the nine-acre Greenbelt Knoll tract in Northeast Philadelphia for $22,200. At the same time, we continued raising the $150,000 in capital required to build the two developments. Sixty-five investors, of whom eight were black, gradually were found to put up the necessary funds. The investors got their money back and earned 6 percent per year on their investments.

Concord Park

Concord Park opened its sales of 139 three- and four-bedroom homes in the $12,000 to $13,600 bracket in August 1954. More than $4,000 spent on advertisements in the daily papers, without indicating that the development was interracial, brought about 25,000 visitors—95 percent white—during the first four months to a model, superbly decorated and furnished by the noted color stylist Beatrice West, who was the interior decorator for Levittown, our major all-white competitor. In addition, the black community spread the word that we were selling houses on an open-occupancy basis, as a result of which approximately two to three thousand black families visited the model by Christmas of 1954. By then about 50 black and 10 white deposits had been secured, although great difficulties had been encountered in answering the questions raised by whites as to what percentage of the development would be occupied by blacks. They were told that our goal was to reflect actual population figures, which, at the time, were 80 percent white and 20 percent black in the Greater Philadelphia area. This explanation failed to satisfy many whites, especially those who recognized the tremendous pressure of the 550,000 blacks in the nine-county Greater Philadelphia area who could not buy at Levittown or Fairless Hills, Pennsylvania, or at any of the hundreds of new developments then being built in the area.

Jane Reinheimer of the American Friends Service Committee's housing staff urged that we set up a controlled occupancy pattern to avoid a ghetto. After almost six months of selling, this was reluctantly voted by our board early in 1955, at a meeting attended by the distinguished black housing leader Dr. Frank Horne, then assistant to the administrator of the Federal Housing and Home Finance Agency. The three black members of the board viewed the quota as a means of fighting segregation, while the white members were divided, some regarding themselves as heroes simply for making housing available to minorities. With the vote of all three black board members and about half of its white members, the quota system was adopted, although my motion to make it half black, half white was amended by Dr. Gray to 55 percent white and 45 percent black to prevent early formation of a black majority. As a result of this move, we found it easier to attract white sales. People accepted our oral assurance that we were determined to achieve a white majority.

One fact became clear: sales to whites are not made easily by salespeople who are themselves unwilling to live in multiracial housing projects. We soon realized that sales commissions had to be geared to securing integration. Once this was done—by changing the commission from $100 for any sale to $100 for white sales and $10 for black sales at a time when we had only seven white and fifty black sales—five white sales were made in five weeks by a salesman who knew nothing of real estate, did not believe in integration, and would refuse himself to move into the new community. This success led me to a major breakthrough, a realization that the formula for securing a substantial increase in sales to whites involved getting a salesman who knew real estate, believed in integration, and *would* live in the community. I called the Housing Opportunities Division of the American Friends Service Committee, proclaiming that somewhere in the United States such a salesman must exist. They found him for us! In the spring of 1955, Stuart E. Wallace, a real estate man in Syracuse, New York, was engaged.[1] He moved into the development, handling the sales with great success: All 139 houses were sold in three years, 55 percent to white buyers and 45 percent to black buyers.

The hardest task was to secure the first ten or twenty white sales. Once this nucleus had been established, it became easier to attract more white buyers. There was no problem as far as black buyers were concerned. Indeed, there were more than an adequate number of applicants with enough cash to buy the homes. The average black family income in the development was about $6,300 per year in 1955, about $350 higher than the average white family income at Concord Park.

---

1. Stuart E. Wallace was until recently head of Fair Housing, Incorporated, a real-estate firm committed to open housing in Cleveland. In 1973, Fair Housing's numerous stockholders sold the firm to Stuart Wallace. It is now named Stuart Wallace Real Estate.

Greenbelt Knoll

At our second development, Greenbelt Knoll, the price range began at $18,000 and $19,000, stabilizing later at $22,500 and higher for three- and five-bedroom contemporary homes. Greenbelt Knoll is on Longford Street at Holme Avenue, a mile and a quarter east of Pennypack Circle, Philadelphia, and there we went through a similar period of difficulty in making the first white sales. However, with the knowledge gained in Concord Park the job proved easier.

There are only nineteen houses on Greenbelt's nine-acre site, and eight of the nineteen houses were sold to blacks. The actual quota was set at one-third black and two-thirds white, a pattern we would have preferred for Concord Park but could not apply, since many sales had been made to blacks before our ratio had been established. Greenbelt Knoll's fine wooded site has parks on four sides, including a two-acre private park which was given to the community association. Swimming and wading pools were built by the Greenbelt Knoll Park Association, and ground was reserved for future tennis courts.

The development has won awards from the City of Philadelphia for "bringing new standards of contemporary residential construction to Philadelphia," and from the American Institute of Architects, as well as fifteen other national groups, for having made "an outstanding contribution to homes for better living." Greenbelt's contemporary homes were designed by architect Robert Bishop of Montgomery & Bishop, who had studied at Taliesen under Frank Lloyd Wright. The post-and-beam houses have a twenty-seven-foot-long glass wall in the living room, with a V-shaped fireplace set into it. Through the glass above the fireplace, one can see the eighty-foot-tall oak and tulip poplars we saved, and the beech and birch trees and the dogwood. At the time of Greenbelt Knoll's construction, bulldozer drivers had been instructed to treat the trees as though they were human beings.

Financing of Concord Park was secured by government-insured

FHA and VA mortgages taken by the Bowery Savings Bank of New York. Similar mortgages, as well as conventional ones, were taken at Greenbelt Knoll by the Nationwide Insurance Company of Columbus, Ohio.

All activities at both Concord Park and Greenbelt Knoll are interracial, from baby-sitting coops and nursery schools to gourmet clubs and various other community gatherings. At Greenbelt, every major sadness or joy is still an occasion for community action or a social get-together.

Princeton Developments

Princeton, New Jersey, is a university town of about eighteen thousand inhabitants which, at one time, had three Presbyterian churches: one for the wealthy Presbyterians, one for the middle-income Presbyterians, and one for the black Presbyterians. One summer, the ministers decided they could have more vacations if they had joint services. Thus, if a Presbyterian decided to get married in the first three weeks of the summer, the marriage ceremony was conducted by a black minister. Despite this startling innovation, nobody left the church. If a Presbyterian died during the first three weeks of the summer, he was buried by a black Presbyterian minister. This, too, caused no defections from the church. On the contrary, the white Presbyterians started making friends with black fellow-churchpeople and discovered there was a certain right that they, as whites, enjoyed in Princeton—namely, the right to buy or rent housing where they pleased—which black Princetonians did not enjoy. As a result, they took the lead in forming the Princeton Housing Group, a loose organization of 130 members of all faiths which, for two years, sought to find houses on the open market. They were able to locate no more than four houses and two building lots, and at this point, they called upon me and my associates to build in Princeton. Two developments were organized under the auspices of the Princeton Housing Associates with slightly over half the capital coming from the Philadelphia group that had invested in Concord Park and Greenbelt Knoll; the rest came from Princetonians, amounting to a total of about $135,000. Two sites were purchased: one just outside Princeton called Glen Acres, a 15-unit development nestled among six white-occupied homes, and another, Maple Crest, a 25-unit development near the Princeton shopping center, in Princeton. Both communities sold easily. About 75 percent of the buyers were white, 25 percent black. No quotas were used, or have been used by us since then.

Modern Community Developers and M-REIT

The obvious success of initial sales at Princeton toward the end of 1957 led to suggestions that I form a national company to develop interracial housing and help builders of such communities with advice, guidance, and financial support. As a result, Modern Community Developers, Incorporated (MCD) was founded in early 1958, with national housing and race relations figures as well as liberal leaders like the late Adlai E. Stevenson and A. Philip Randolph endorsing and encouraging it.

Modern Community Developers began work in eight states. Soon, however, MCD hit a major roadblock: Deerfield, Illinois, an all-white suburb of Chicago, condemned the company's two separate sites and designated them for public parks in order to keep the village all white. To meet the challenge of the Deerfield Freedom of Residence battle, the MCD board was enlarged by the addition of Eleanor Roosevelt; Xerox-inventor Chester L. Carlson; Eliot D. Pratt, Chairman of Goddard College and publisher of *Current;* James Farmer, founder and first National Director of the Congress of Racial Equality (CORE); Willard Wirtz, Adlai E. Stevenson's law partner, later to be Secretary of Labor; Dorothy Height, President of the National Council of Negro Women; journalist Andrew Norman, and others of note.

The court battle, recounted in the previous chapter, ripped the silken curtain from the virtual total exclusion of blacks from white suburbia. It was fought for almost four years by a legal team headed by Adlai Stevenson's law firm, with leading roles played by Willard Wirtz, Newton Minow, John W. Hunt, Jr., John Morris, and, later, Joseph L. Rauh, Jr., as chief counsel. The attorney general, Robert Kennedy, was urged to file a brief *amicus* prepared by his staff, but he declined. In mid-1963, the battle was finally lost when the U.S. Supreme Court refused to hear the case.

When the MCD board saw the handwriting on the wall in the Deerfield battle in 1961, they voted to stop building new communities. Clearly, the courts were not about to challenge exclusionary rezoning practices, and the board decided instead to buy existing apartment houses in good neighborhoods, far from ghettos and open to all. This program resulted in the acquisition, through limited partnerships, of three large buildings, totalling 633 apartments in the Washington, D.C.–Maryland area.

The first building paid a cash flow of about 4.6 percent a year for the first nine and a half years of ownership. The second building in Washington, D.C., was set up very conservatively with an unusual sinking fund to amortize a balloon payment due on expiration of the mortgage. For this reason, in part at least, it has paid very little cash flow since its acquisition in 1964. The third property, purchased in 1964 in Maryland, has paid no cash flow to investors, who received instead an average of $237 per year tax shelter per $1,000 investment for the first seven and a half years.

The first two buildings also provided tax shelter for their investors, on an average of $73 a year for the first building and $58 a year on $1,000 investment for the second year, giving investors tax-free spendable cash. In addition, all three buildings have substantially amortized mortages: if a building were sold at a reasonable price, investors would make a taxable profit on their investment; if it were refinanced, investors could get non-taxable cash. In 1977, one of the buildings was sold at a capital gain of $2,635 per $1,000 invested.

MCD concentrated its efforts on developing its apartment-house programs along with one of its subsidiaries, Planned Communities,

Incorporated (PC), with which it merged. In 1963, PC began to organize M-REIT (the Mutual Real Estate Investment Trust), in the hope that it would be a source of profit for the pioneering investors in MCD, now renamed Planned Communities, Incorporated. Since it was not possible to merge a corporation with a real-estate investment trust, it was agreed that Planned Communities would distribute its assets to its investors, and that some of its board members would be added to the M-REIT board immediately, more as vacancies occurred. The liquidation of Planned Communities is now complete, with investors receiving $3.01 per new PC share. Investors in the original Modern Community Developers, which took the brunt of the tremendous beating in the Deerfield Freedom of Residence battle, suffered a substantial loss in liquidation, receiving no more than $18.06 per $100 they had invested. However, investors who came in when Planned Communities was formed as a partially owned subsidiary of MCD, got $63.21 per $100 invested, in addition to one modest dividend and a small profit on any original common stock they held.

M-REIT, officially established in 1965, is a publicly owned company which buys apartment houses far from areas of minority concentration, using affirmative marketing to establish and maintain ethnically diverse communities. It has over eight thousand investors who put in about $12 million, controlling approximately $40 million in assets, that is, apartment houses with roughly 3,400 units in ten states.

According to M-REIT's 1970 report, 5.2 percent of their residents were black. No serious white flight had occurred in any of their buildings, only two of which had more than a 15 percent black occupancy (one 17 percent, another 19 percent), while most of the others had less than 10 percent. In 1972, M-REIT's properties had approximately 8 percent minority residents, which had risen to 11 percent by 1973.

Some of M-REIT's apartment houses have been sold by now, generally at a profit. During a period of roughly three years of M-REIT ownership, one of the buildings in St. Louis changed from zero percent to 24 percent black occupancy. Nevertheless, it was sold at a cash flow profit of $328,000, that is, equal to 33 percent of the cash required to buy this almost four-hundred-unit development.

The author was manager of M-REIT until 1969, when he lost control of the Trust.[2] While M-REIT's 3 percent nontaxable distributions continued for several years, M-REIT, like other real estate investment trusts, suffered from the effects of inflation, the energy crisis, and a faltering economy. In 1974, the executive staff was replaced. Since then M-REIT's financial situation has begun to improve.

Other Integrated Communities

University Heights, Providence, R.I.

At University Heights, for the first time in the United States, a private developer successfully combined economic and racial integration in a 500-unit garden apartment–townhouse–shopping center complex. By 1973, over 350 families, about 20 percent of them black, lived in this community. Economic integration was achieved by placing the buildings around courtyards and financing some of them with FHA standard interest rate loans under Section 220 of the National Housing Act and others with 3 percent loans under Section 221 (d) (3). This kind of site plan allows people of all economic levels to live side by side in almost identical apartments, although some rents are subsidized while others conform to current market rates. University Heights is situated in an urban renewal area about a mile from downtown Providence, and about a mile from the college community of Pembroke and Brown. It is on a major highway, surrounded on three sides by a small, black neighborhood and on the fourth side by commercial establishments. It is close to an upper-middle-class white neighborhood, one of the finest in the city of Providence.

2. As a result, he left M-REIT to organize Partners in Housing.

The project was suggested to the late Irving Fain by Modern Community Developers, on whose board he served, in response to recommendations of the local fair-housing leadership. The initial market analysis showing feasibility, subject to the provision of recreational amenities, was made by Louis Winnick and Frank Kristof. Fain, a leading Providence industrialist, became the first president of University Heights, imparting to the business and social leadership of the new community great energy, rare vision, and financial strength.

With the completion of its third section of 100 units—now under construction as a condominium under the guidance of Lyle Fain, the founder's son—University Heights will have almost five hundred families in two- and three-story buildings ranged around a series of small, attractively landscaped courtyards.

Children of varying racial and economic backgrounds play together in each of the courtyards of the first two sections. Neither they nor trained observers could easily tell the difference between the two types of houses around them, that is, those built with 221 (d) (3) loans, in which families with incomes of about $4,500 to $9,000 live, and those built under the standard interest rate (FHA Section 220), where families with incomes from about $7,000 to $25,000 and higher live.

In all exteriors the two types of garden apartment buildings are similar, although the market-rental apartments are somewhat larger than the moderate-rental ones—1,530 square feet for a three-bedroom townhouse and 1,187 square feet for a moderate rental three-bedroom apartment. Although the higher-rent apartments have several additional amenities, the basic features are identical. In 1973, the three-bedroom luxury townhouse rented for about $300, while the rentals for three-bedroom apartments ranged from $170 to $190, and about $290 for three-bedroom luxury apartments.[3]

3. In 1976, rent for the three-bedroom luxury townhouse rose to $400 and to $325 for the three-bedroom luxury apartments. Rentals for middle-income three-bedroom apartments range from $210 to $250.

In the first two sections, the market-rent apartments and town-houses are financed with standard interest mortgages, the middle-income apartments with 3 percent mortgages.

Interviews with University Heights tenants, and with visitors and staff at the shopping center, showed that some whites tend to exaggerate the percentage of blacks in residence, often guessing at a figure as high as 50 to 70 percent, when the actual percentage is no more than 15 to 20 percent.

Investigations revealed that it seemed easier for the community's white and black families in the upper-income housing to accept black middle-income rather than white middle-income families as neighbors. This can be explained, in part, by a greater mobility of black residents in the $4,500 to $9,000 income bracket in contrast to the more stationary position of white families in the same income range. In other words, acceptance seems more related to social class and upward mobility than to race.

Fieldstondale Coop, Riverdale, Bronx, New York

Fieldstondale, a 180-unit cooperative consisting of two high-rise fireproof buildings, was built without subsidy under FHA Section 213 and partially financed by Modern Community Developers. Prior to MCD's participation, the prospective buyers were almost all white. However, as a result of affirmative marketing techniques, vigorously conducted to secure black residents by informing minority families—as well as all MCD stockholders—of the opportunity to live in a country-like setting near the Hudson, only a short trip from midtown Manhattan, the community was successfully integrated. This was not accomplished without encountering the inevitable objections, in particular the builders' fear that the sight of "so many" nonwhites among initial move-ins might hurt the sales. After discussing this issue openly, the Coop Board concluded that the problem was far less insuperable than the builders believed it to be. At the same time, the developer appealed to MCD to try at least to delay initial minority move-ins lest they weaken the white sales effort. MCD was able to convince the developer that the presence of minority families would not interfere to any serious degree with the selling of the apartments. Through good staff work by the developer, and small briefing sessions where whites met their prospective neighbors, the Coop Board moved ahead toward establishing an interracial community without incidents or adverse effects on sales in virtually all-white Riverdale. Shortly after Fieldstondale's initial occupancy, about 10 percent of its residents were nonwhite.

Large meetings of potential residents remained one of Fieldstondale's most effective ways of recruiting. Some of the most interested participants at such meetings subsequently became members of the Coop Board, while most of the original Coop directors moved into the apartments three or four years later. In order to defuse any possible future conflicts, some clustering of black sales that had occurred on certain floors was discouraged prior to move-ins.

The Coop sales were unquestionably aided by good site planning, good design, and equally good construction by competent builders. To this should be added the attractive site, with its 10-mile view over Van Cortlandt Park on one side and the Palisades on the other. At the time, in 1960, one-bedroom apartments sold for $1,877 with carrying charges of $119 and up, while two-bedroom apartments began at $2,627 with carrying costs of $159 and up.

Runnymede

Runnymede, in Hockessin, a suburb of Wilmington, Delaware, is a 29-lot development which we organized in 1958, in cooperation with a Quaker-led Delaware group. A year later, Modern Community Developers invested $25,000, and local people about three times that amount, to set up what the Wilmington, Delaware, *Journal* described in its issue of November 17, 1959, as "a controlled housing development with a maximum Negro occupancy of 25 percent." Runnymede was the last of three communities where my associates and I thought the use of quotas advisable to insure the racially balanced character of the development.

The site, a twenty-three-acre tract of land, was subdivided into twenty-nine lots with two acres set aside for a park area. Essentially, Runnymede was a custom development, that is, lots were sold to 23 families, three of whom were black. Most of these families made their own building arrangements. By 1974, there were twenty homes in existence or under construction, ranging in value from $30,000 to $35,000 and more. Some sold for less, and a few would sell for far more today.

The residents include a lawyer, a doctor, a policeman, teachers, engineers, chemists, accountants, and a salesman. During the early days, residents got a cool reception from their neighbors, some of whom would not permit their children to babysit for members of the Runnymede community. This coolness soon wore off, and, in fact, the neighborhood has been unusually stable, with only three of the original buyers moving away. Since the black demand at Runnymede fell below the anticipated level, the quota system, which had been adopted in response to fears of local whites that an all-black development had been planned, could have been dispensed with.

Altogether, the Runnymede Corporation raised $81,950 in equity financing from fifty-two stockholders, the major one being Modern Community Developers (Planned Communities). The Corporation continued in business until October 1972, when a plan of liquidation was adopted. At the end of November, 1972, the Corporation was dissolved, with stockholders receiving a profit in the form of capital gain of 7.2 percent on their investments in Runnymede.

Glover Park Apartments

Glover Park Apartments, a 73-unit, four-story, elevator, hillside building facing the Archbold-Glover Parkway near fashionable

Georgetown in Washington, D.C., was purchased by a limited partnership organized by Planned Communities in 1962.

Before the building was purchased, a study by the Social Science Research Bureau had revealed that 16 percent of the residents threatened to move if the building were integrated, while 10 percent said they would consider moving. However, when the first black families moved into the building, none of the white residents left.

The black demand at this building, whose location is somewhat peripheral, remained very modest for the first eight years of ownership. As a result, the percentages of black residents were generally under 6 percent. In 1970, however, the percentages started moving up, and by 1976, the building was about 12 percent black. There has been no white flight and no diminution of heavy white demand.

The Glover Park experience confirmed that the key to securing integration in residential buildings is clearly not whether a manager is black or white. In fact, a black manager proved as unsuccessful in increasing integration at Glover Park Apartments as previous white managers did. What does matter and is crucial is the social concern of a manager, his or her regard for others, which alone can transform an apartment house into a warm, truly integrated community.

Like any other rental property, Glover Park Apartments had to adjust its rents to keep pace with rising prices. In May 1974, rentals including utilities ranged from $181 and up for one-bedroom apartments, to $215 and up for two-bedroom apartments, increasing to $200 and $242, respectively, by 1976.

The Highlands, Washington, D.C.

In January 1964, The Highlands, a 145-unit, eight-story, fire-proof structure built in 1912 was purchased by Modern Community Developers (now Planned Communities—PC) through a limited partnership. It is located on Washington, D.C.'s traditionally fashionable, all-white Connecticut Avenue, opposite the Washington Hilton Hotel and the city's largest office-building complex, Universal North and South. The Highlands, which had been modernized six years earlier, did not attract a substantial nonwhite demand: for the first six years, blacks made up less than 5 percent of the residents. In 1970, however, non-white demand began to increase so that by mid-1971 the building was about 12 percent black, with a similar percentage of Spanish-speaking families. In addition, about 12 percent of the families were foreign diplomats or foreign nationals of countries including India, Vietnam, and Korea. The equivalent figures for 1976 are 16 percent, 14 percent and 11 percent, respectively. In 1974, the rents ranged from $139 and up for the 104 efficiency apartments and from $162 and up for the 40 one-bedroom apartments, with a large penthouse efficiency renting for somewhat more. The rooms are unusually large, with high ceilings and air conditioning. It has been observed, however, that many blacks, kept out of high-quality housing for years, prefer newer apartments with much smaller rooms at higher rents than those in older buildings in better locations.

Rosemary Village

In June 1964, a limited partnership organized by Modern Community Developers (now PC), with myself as general partner, bought Rosemary Village, a 415-unit garden apartment and townhouse complex on a fifteen-acre site in Silver Spring, Maryland, just across the District of Columbia line. That year, the first black families began to move into this previously all-white community, the first apartment house to be deliberately integrated south of the Mason-Dixon Line.

There was no white flight: only about six of the families which moved out during the next few years gave integration as a reason. By 1966, thirty-eight black families lived in Rosemary. By mid-1973, Rosemary was somewhat over one-third black; in 1976, with strong white demand continuing, it was half black.

A study of Rosemary Village, which Roger N. Beilenson and I

conducted in 1968 for the National Commission on Urban Problems, disclosed the following facts:

1. Whites were generally willing to move into an apartment house knowing there were black residents;
2. Few whites moved into Rosemary Village because of its ethnic diversity;
3. The black residents seemed to be of a higher social class than the whites, with incomes definitely above white incomes;
4. The large majority of whites and blacks found integrated living pleasant; few had any trouble they attributed to race;
5. There was substantial social contact between the races. Of the seventy-one interviewed, twenty-nine never visited neighbors for a social evening, seventeen had visited blacks, and twenty-four had visited whites only. Of the thirty-four blacks, twelve had not visited whites, and four had visited blacks only. Since blacks composed only one-seventh of the tenants when the study was made, the fact that about one-quarter of the whites had visited blacks is a mark of considerable interracial contact;
6. About thirteen of the seventy-one whites interviewed exhibited considerable prejudice against blacks; a few of them had moved in after blacks became tenants. A number of other whites made statements such as: "They keep to themselves and we keep to ourselves."

The area around Rosemary Village, formerly all white, has now become integrated. A fairly large number of white families, in addition to some black families from Rosemary, have moved into the adjacent neighborhood. Houses in this area are in heavy demand, with prices moving upward at a fast pace.

Rosemary Village, with attractive ivy-covered buildings and many flower and vegetable gardens kept by the townhouse residents, has a well-kept swimming pool area with a second pool for children. There is a deck that can be used for dancing and a pavilion which can be turned into a bandstand. There is space for eating, drinking, games, and sunbathing. The community has more than twenty landscaped play areas, many with children's equipment colorfully painted by either the residents' association or the management.

In 1973, during a period of about eight months, Rosemary

Village discontinued its ads in the *Washington Post*. When the ads were resumed toward the end of 1973, white demand increased substantially. During the same ad-less period, word of mouth about Rosemary resulted in heavy minority demand. In addition, move-outs following rental increases due to inflationary pressure indicated conclusively that Rosemary's black residents, who have far fewer housing choices than their white counterparts, were less likely to leave.

In 1973, rents ranged from $191 for a one-bedroom apartment, $235 for a two-bedroom apartment, to $271 for a three-bedroom townhouse. By 1976, rents had increased to $229, $278, and $325, respectively, including utilities.

Lake Meadows and Prairie Shores

Ferd Kramer, a Chicago housing developer and head of Draper & Kramer, mortgage bankers and realtors, is one of the nation's most socially concerned mortgage bankers. His group owns two major integrated developments in Chicago's South Side urban renewal area, in the heart of the ghetto.

One of these developments is Lake Meadows. Its hundred-acre site, with ten buildings ranging from 12 to 21 stories with 2,009 apartments, was originally owned and managed by the New York Life Insurance Company. Rents started at $85, going up to $450 a month in 1967. Occupancy of the first apartment building in 1953 was about 99 percent nonwhite, but the last building, a high-rent luxury structure completed in 1960, was about 25 percent nonwhite. Over all, the residents of Lake Meadows are about 88 percent nonwhite.

The other development, adjacent to Lake Meadows, is Prairie Shores, consisting of 1,700 apartments in five high-rise buildings financed under the FHA 220 Program. Rentals began in 1958 and were completed in 1961, with rents ranging from about $85 to $220. In 1973, a one-bedroom apartment rented for $136.50 to $184 and a two-bedroom apartment for $185 to $233. Originally

71

Prairie Shores, developed and managed by Draper & Kramer in conjunction with the nearby Michael Reese Hospital, had a definite plan for maintaining a two-thirds-white–to–one-third-black housing pattern. By 1971, this ratio had changed to approximately 20 to 25 percent black. Ferd Kramer believes that balanced integration generally cannot be achieved without the use of occupancy controls or quotas, and feels quotas should be legalized.

Great care was taken in the initial rentals at Prairie Shores to assure integration. Once an integrated pattern had been established, there were no major problems in keeping it. In fact, white demand for the apartments has been high ever since, especially from families without children, in an area where schools are virtually all black.

The success of Lake Meadows and Prairie Shores in the heart of a large ghetto seems to be based on the following factors:

1. Affirmative marketing. The original intention of the New York Life Insurance Company was to give preference to blacks. New York Life's Director of Management at that time, Elmer Chase, signed a personal covenant of open occupancy in his Presbyterian church in Princeton, and decided to give instructions to local managers to make vigorous efforts to recruit white renters. This was done partly in recognition of the fact that the black renting market might not support the planned 2,000 units, and because some difficulties had been experienced in filling the first 590 apartments. In addition, Draper & Kramer were planning to house staff members of the Michael Reese Hospital, which bordered Lake Meadows, at Prairie Shores. It was hoped that this new development would reflect the interracial composition of the staff. As George and Eunice Grier pointed out in *Privately Developed Interracial Housing,* "heavily Negro Lake Meadows, it was felt, would make this goal much more difficult to achieve, since it would indicate a solidification of the segregated pattern in the area;"
2. A new school was built to serve Lake Meadows and Prairie Shores;
3. Aggressive promotion directed toward whites was carried over "good music" radio stations, and financial assistance was extended in the form of free rent for an apartment on a lower floor while the tenants waited for their upper-floor apartment to be finished.

4. Lake Meadows and Prairie Shores were large enough to create their own neighborhood unit, complete with shopping center. On one side, they were separated from the ghetto by a wide boulevard-like street; on the other side, they faced the lake;
5. Lake Meadows and Prairie Shores were both anchored to a major medical institution, the Michael Reese Hospital;
6. Draper & Kramer counted among their staff a substantial group of people with deep social concerns—not only Ferd Kramer, but also Harry Gottlieb, their mortgage manager, and others who worked hard and dared to try what most housing developers would have said was impossible: the development of a profitable interracial community in the heart of a poverty-stricken ghetto. This goal was achieved because of careful planning and hard work, and the recognition that the problems of housing for major institutions cannot be solved except within the framework of truly interracial communities.

Prairie Shores has been paying its investors at approximately 8 percent per year in cash flow. According to Ferd Kramer, his companies' similarly planned efforts have been equally profitable.

Hepzibah Homes, Providence, R.I.

Hepzibah, a Hebrew word for "perfect city," or "doing something with the whole of one's heart," was organized by Irving Jay Fain in 1965 with the following goals:

1. To demonstrate that property values do not decline when a black family moves into an all-white area;
2. To show that whites will not flee from two- or three-family homes when a black moves in;
3. To demonstrate that racially integrated housing can be sociologically and economically successful and can be operated routinely without special effort or expense;
4. To promote racial integration in Greater Providence;
5. To improve housing;
6. To improve the availability of housing in Greater Providence;
7. To arrest housing neglect;
8. To retain racial integration in neighborhoods subject to racial change;
9. To provide safe, sanitary, efficient, attractive, and modern housing for families with modest incomes.

Translating goals into action, Hepzibah adopted the following procedure:

1. To buy two- or three-family houses in desirable neighborhoods currently all white;
2. To rehabilitate housing and maintain it carefully;
3. To create additional housing by conversion of incomplete third floors;
4. To arrest deterioration, where feasible, by acquiring several houses close together;
5. To attempt to preserve one vacancy in each building for a black family;
6. To reserve vacancies occurring in houses occupied by a black family for a white family, thus retaining integration;
7. To reserve vacancies for whites on blocks where there is a threat of change from white to thoroughly black occupancy;
8. To seek out lower-cost housing that can be improved within the price range of lower-income families;
9. To subject each acquisition to a careful scrutiny for economic feasibility.

The Hepzibah Company balance sheet of April 30, 1971, showed that buildings had been acquired for about 1.5 million dollars. Rental income at that time was $18,600 a month.

When Irving J. Fain, the founder of Hepzibah, died in August 1970, the Company owned about fifty houses with approximately 150 dwelling units. Almost all were two- or three-family houses, except 2 four-family, 1 single-family, 1 six-family, and 1 twelve-family dwelling. In April 1968, 35 of the 133 apartments were occupied by black families, with two vacancies expressly reserved for occupancy by blacks. In the opinion of the Hepzibah Company, reservation according to race is consistent with the intent of the Rhode Island Fair Housing Law.

Originally the Hepzibah Company concentrated purchases on the east side of Providence in the city's most desirable area, which, although all white, is close to a black area. East side houses were purchased for $15,000 to $25,000, with rents ranging from $60 to $175 without heat or utilities. Most houses rented for $100 to $135. Later, however, houses were acquired over much of the Greater Providence area, with a few homes on the fringe of the

South Providence ghetto. In order to achieve racial stability and maintain high physical standards, Hepzibah upgraded and integrated the newly purchased buildings.

In the beginning, the Company managed its housing through a local real estate broker, Rotkin and Sidney, but later decided to manage their holdings directly. These houses, rehabilitated to a sound and attractive condition, generally became some of the most desirable homes on the block.

By and large, the reaction to integration was positive: tenant relations were usually cordial, and in only two cases did white tenants oppose their black neighbors. (In one instance, the families became friendly, and in the other, the black family was acccepted by the neighbors in general, and the white family, feeling somewhat excluded, tried to become friendly.) A change like this is most effectively brought about when blacks move into a white neighborhood as part of a program that includes the upgrading of housing developments. Such programs, more than anything else, are likely to turn white resistance to blacks into white acceptance of black neighbors, chiefly because white opposition is almost always based on black stereotypes which the new residents simply do not resemble.

In most cases, white families moving into Hepzibah knew they would have some black fellow-residents. However, no white family, including the two who raised objections, ever moved out because a black family moved in.

The rents at Hepzibah were set at 1.25 percent per month of the total cost of the houses, including improvements.

Starting in 1971, the Company began selling the Hepzibah properties. This process has now been completed. It is hoped that the new owners will maintain integration not only as a well-functioning, established pattern but also because people got used to it.

Gienclift, San Diego, California

That nothing is impossible in the field of race relations and housing was demonstrated by the example of the Prairie Shores—

Lake Meadows developments mentioned earlier. The story of Glenclift in San Diego, California, points in the same direction. A 316-unit rental development, it was built as FHA Title 9 Defense Housing. It opened in December 1953 and was primarily rented to blacks. A year later, Glenclift had over 50 percent vacancies, and many units had been damaged by vandalism. As a result, the tract soon became known as a black slum. In 1955, the tract was sold, and seven months later the new owners could claim 100-percent occupancy: at higher rents than before, but two-thirds white and one-third black.

The key to the successful reversal of a downward trend might very well be attributed "to a market upswing, but mainly to resourceful and aggressive management with heavy promotion to whites," as George and Eunice Grier state in *Privately Developed Interracial Housing*.

When I visited Glenclift in 1958, I was taken on a tour by the real-estate executive, Mrs. Christine Kleponis, who had effected the change. Earlier—as far as I could find out—when Mrs. Kleponis took over the management of the property, she had started evicting some black families in order to make the community all white. Her reason for doing so was her view that some blacks did not care properly for the development's grounds or buildings. However, she soon discovered to her surprise that many whites were willing to rent rehabilitated units next door to blacks. Hence she quickly shifted gears, organizing block parties and arranging for loans of tools and gifts of shrubs and seed to families who would use them. In less than seven months, she had managed not only to fill the buildings at higher rentals (two-thirds white and one-third black) but was elected to the boards of directors of the local NAACP and Urban League!

Fortunately, Mrs. Kleponis did not ask *me* whether it was possible to integrate this previously all-black development. Inevitably, I believe, my reply would have been rather discouraging. Although Glenclift was probably the choicest rental location in the area, the fact that 150 units were occupied by blacks and only one by a white family at the time her firm took title to the 158 buildings (each with two side-by-side two-bedroom apartments) would have convinced me that integration could not possibly be achieved. Now I know better.

The Pitfalls

Pitfalls in the development of interracial housing are, in many cases, no different from those which threaten the development of any new housing.

Poor land planning and bad architectural design, poor color styling, poor furnishing of the model, and lack of excellent merchandising can be very costly in terms of winning approval for integrated housing. In addition, a local builder's lack of economic strength can be most damaging.

One of the most serious dangers that an interracial project can face is lack of capital. This may be caused partly by delays—routine in the building industry—that can be considerably increased by local opposition, as the earlier examples demonstrate. The developer needs the courage to ask for, and work for, adequate capital so that delays and obstructions represent no major problems in meeting his bills.

Another pitfall developers of open-occupancy housing must avoid is hiring real-estate people—black or white—who say they believe in open housing and then proceed with the marketing on a virtually uniracial basis. In this case, verbal assurance is simply not a useful indication of salespeople's concern for truly open communities. A developer should ask for more concrete assurances, based on past performance which demonstrate beyond doubt that the real-estate person is deeply committed to a *policy* of establishing multiracial housing. Then compensation should be tied to the achievement of business and social goals.

In some cases, it is more than easy to develop a uniracial community, an accomplishment hardly deserving high commissions. In my experience, economic determinism has a key way of affecting sales: if you give equal commissions for easy as well as tough sales, only the easy sales will be made in quantity. At the same time, the staff handling difficult sales and rentals must understand that in order to reach groups most in need of housing, the technique of affirmative marketing must be used—not quotas.

Poor site selection is another obstacle that faces a developer of multiracial housing, in particular the selection of sites in minority areas, or in the path of minority expansion. Such sites may well lead to the rise of future ghettos. The key to site selection for all housing, and certainly for integrated housing, is a careful study of the location, a fact which cannot be stressed too strongly.

Of all the pitfalls in the path of a developer of multiracial communities, zoning represents the greatest danger. "The conversion of zoning from a tool to a weapon," indicates a "shift from overt discrimination to more subtle forms of regulation and restriction."[4] Many areas, as is well known, have been deliberately closed *de facto* to most minority groups by the simple use of zoning, which effectively keeps out low- and modest-income families.

Recent decisions of the Pennsylvania Supreme Court may help to open suburban areas to low- and moderate-cost housing construction. The court ruled that Concord Township, in Delaware County, cannot use exclusionary zoning in the form of two- and three-acre minimum lot sizes to avoid making housing available to lower-income families.

In a second decision, the court declared that Nether Providence Township, in the same county, cannot zone against apartments simply because the township does not want to face the problems associated with such use. This does not mean that minimum lot sizes are out. On the contrary, the court ruled that lot sizes must be reasonable, consistent with physical factors related to that parcel of land, and compatible with trends and the indicated highest best use for the land. Arbitrary lot sizes, if aimed at excluding people, are prohibited.

4. A. S. Lazerow. "Discriminatory Zoning: Legal Battleground of the Seventies," in G. Sternlieb and V. Paulus, eds., *Housing, 1971–72* (New York: AMS Press, 1974), p. 70.

Even in New Jersey, with its affluent white suburbs, the walls of privilege may soon be breached. In March 1975, the State Supreme Court struck down a number of local ordinances whose large-lot zoning requirements prevent low- and moderate-income groups—mostly minority families—from living in the suburbs. The court further declared that "every developing suburban community in the state must provide for its 'fair share' of the housing needs of its surrounding region."[5] While this in itself is no guarantee that low-cost housing will become available, the court's decision is bound to serve as a precedent for fair-housing groups who seek to establish open housing in open suburbs nationwide.

A major sign of the future is the U.S. Supreme Court's 1976 ruling in *Hills* v. *Gautreaux,* a Chicago-based case that had spent ten years in the courts. The decision permits federal courts to order the construction of low-income public housing in now-white suburbs in order to alleviate racial segregation in cities. Although its impact may not be evident for years, the decision's promise is far-reaching: by implication, it places the issue of school segregation squarely where it belongs—in the legacy of our racially segregated housing patterns. If the government, the housing industry, and the consumer will act *affirmatively now* to create and maintain logical open housing patterns across the country, our now-white suburbs will be spared the flight-and-resegregation pattern which is still consuming our cities.

The problems of zoning,[6] and how they affect builders whose aim is to provide truly open housing for families of low or middle income, are major and complex. These warnings will provide some examples of their range:

1. Whenever possible, the site should be bought subject to zoning and subdivision approval and building permits. Without such safeguards, the developer may find himself saddled with a costly

5. *Philadelphia Inquirer,* March 30, 1975.
6. For more on the subject of zoning, see Suburban Action Institute, pp. 116–121.

piece of ground. Under no circumstances should the seller be granted any right to approve the site planning or architectural designs;

2. The agreement of sale should state clearly the seller's responsibility to aid in every way the securing of zoning and subdivision approvals, of water, sewer, and building permits, and of whatever else needs official authorization;

3. The architectural drawings should not give any indication of the type of financing or names of principals. A separate entity for each major job, without stating their social purpose, is the best way to get jobs done;

4. Probably the most promising way of providing housing in areas of high opposition to open occupancy or low- or middle-income housing is to work with a local builder acceptable to the authorities on projects large enough to make it worth his while to risk their displeasure;

5. At no point should an effort be made to inform the authorities in advance of the long-range social purpose of the project—in my case, the development of interracial housing. This error was committed in Deerfield, Illinois, where we told a local minister of our plans and asked him to break the news to the community. His opposition led to the uproar that stopped construction just a few weeks before the roads would have been completed and the models opened to the public, a time when condemnation for parks would have been rather difficult. The law makes it clear that housing is open to everybody: it is not necessary to ask permission. The best education a community can receive is to see black and white families living together successfully.

Buying Apartment Buildings to Open Closed Housing

If the goal is to achieve open housing in virtually closed areas, it is vital to select white neighborhoods which are both far from minority areas and not in the path of minority expansion. Undertaking a new project just a block or two, or three, away from the ghetto, or even half a mile distant, may merely postpone the date on which an integrated development becomes swallowed up in an expanding ghetto. The ideal solution is to seek housing in the midst of a substantial number of other apartment houses in white suburban sections.

In general, there should be some minority market potential. Unless the major city of the metropolitan area is 3 percent or slightly more nonwhite, there is a possibility of minority demand being so small as to make meaningful integration unlikely.

Ventures are more likely to succeed in high growth-rate areas, and it is essential to maintain special efforts to find property in such areas through frequent contacts with brokers and owners.

The key to success in owning and managing an interracial apartment house is often dependent on its *location* in a city or county known to have good schools. Equally important are nearness to transportation, schools, shopping, and other amenities.

One of the key pitfalls for a group determined to buy open-housing apartment buildings is becoming wedded to a single area just because it is close to the home base. A New York-based operation, for example, could hurt itself tremendously by concentrating on New York's rent-controlled buildings, properties that already have difficulties meeting their bills under stringent rent controls and fantastic red tape. It is far better to avoid such properties and initiate action in several economically more favorable areas, without naming them publicly. Paying too much for a building in order to achieve one's social and business goals is another error to be avoided, as is the weakening of one's bargaining power for price and financing terms by premature publicity about social goals. Occasionally, an owner may even refuse to sell, especially if he has other property near the site or the buildings a buyer is interested in.

Sometimes buyers, in their eagerness to close a specific deal, fail to insist on a full financial disclosure on the part of the owner. When an owner refuses inspection of the financial reports on his property, the buyer must check and recheck every item with great care, and obtain proof of actual income and expenses at closing.

Another common error is to take title to property in the form of a corporation, when the form of a limited partnership would cope more successfully with tax problems. In most instances, a corporate structure fails to meet the specific tax needs of the owners, with the result that hundreds of thousands of dollars of tax shelter may be lost by not making use of a limited partnership vehicle.

In a limited partnership, the depreciation on the building flows through to each partner proportionately to his investment. Thus, for the first six or seven years, and often longer, a rental property will throw off substantial tax shelter to investors. For example, an investor (or limited partner) in the 50-percent tax bracket who may get a tax loss of $300 per year per $1,000 invested for the first six or seven years can have the equivalent of about $150 per year of tax-free spendable income. For a person in the 33-percent tax bracket, that tax loss is equivalent to $100 a year of tax-free spendable income. Had the property been owned by a corporation, the tax shelter would have been lost.

The liability of a limited partner, like that of a stockholder in a corporation, is restricted to his investment. However, if a corporation has a bad year and its stock goes down in value, the shareholder has to sell his stock if he wishes to take the loss off his income tax. If a limited partnership has a bad year, this is reflected in a higher tax shelter, which means more tax-free spendable cash for the investor who is sheltering other income from taxes. The substantial tax advantage that a limited partnership provides can, therefore, make the difference between a venture's economic success and failure.

Another error a prospective buyer must avoid is buying the lowest rental building in the area. While rents in such a building may seem to be the only ones blacks can afford, its acquisition will also, for this very reason, complicate the maintenance of a truly interracial community.

Groups who organize for the purpose of buying open housing must establish clear social and business goals. A suggested list might include:

1. The creation of new open communities in white areas far from ghettos;
2. The creation of new and open communities in minority areas;
3. The strengthening of existing multiracial communities by buying

in areas with active, integrated neighborhood associations, which might also help with locating apartment houses for sale.

The first of the goals is the easiest to attain. The second can best be pursued by acquiring large sites—preferably a mile or a mile and a half square—where new towns-in-town can be built. We need the courage to recreate the advantages of a town in the heart of a city. But all three goals should be pursued simultaneously if we are to apply the ideals we profess.

Developing and Maintaining an Integrated Community

In my pioneer communities—Concord Park and Greenbelt Knoll, both in the Philadelphia area, and later Runnymede in Hockessin, a suburb of Wilmington, Delaware—interracial occupancy was established by using a quota system. By 1958, we had discarded quotas as a means of creating racially balanced communities. Instead, we relied more and more on affirmative marketing to end segregation in housing, aided by years of experience and knowledge of the housing market.

Importance of a Committed Staff

We have observed the value of a staff that cares enough about integration to live in the community they are promoting.

It is vital for the staff, black and white, to be briefed on the problem of pent-up minority demand before they embark on rentals and sales. Often in an area where minority demand may create no more than a 20-percent minority community, early demand from minorities may be such that unless thoughtful concern for securing an interracial community guides all activities, the first rentals could be overwhelmingly to minority families, thus discouraging white demand and seriously endangering the economic and social success of the community.

Without turning away any qualified minority customers, it is important to persuade some minority families to wait for housing in order to redress the temporary imbalance which would run counter to the aim of developing a truly integrated community. If this is done with tact and care, problems are unlikely to arise, for the overwhelming majority of blacks are eager to demonstrate that open housing works.

Avoid Being Labeled a "Minority Community"

Once the social goals have been set, work hard to imprint on the minds of the community your fine planning, housing, and other practical attributes. The reputation of a community with first-rate contemporary architecture and excellent recreational facilities soon overshadows the possibilities of identification as "that integrated community." If people talk admiringly about your community's fine features, the subject of race takes on the incidental perspective it deserves.

To assure such excellence, it is vital to select a fine architect and an imaginative planner, or a firm engaged in both architecture and planning. Preference should be given to local firms. It is also wise to have the team of architect and planners participate in the site selection *before* negotiating or signing the sales agreement. Inform the team of the acreage needed for your purposes, and make sure they are familiar with local subdivision ordinances and the general problems of zoning, utilities, and other matters, such as the minimum acreage for a planned unit development, that might well be conditions of the sales agreement.

Affirmative Marketing

In developing a new community in white suburbia, it is essential to reach the market of those who believe in an open society and multiracial living. This contact can best be established through:

1. *Good music stations.* There is usually at least one, and sometimes several, in major metropolitan areas;
2. *Liberal radio commentators.* Some in major cities have talk shows that run from 11 P.M. to 2 A.M., and advertising time is fairly easy to buy. Interviews are also available without cost. If no black demand appears, try radio stations beamed at black audiences. Most major cities have at least one;
3. *Television.* Although this is more costly, it enables a developer to show exciting pictures of the community, promising, if the development is really photogenic, the most profitable response;
4. *Liberal newspapers and magazines on the local or national level.* Both help attract people to your communities;
5. *Small inexpensive advertisements repeated regularly,* thus developing a clientele which, combined with that found through the preceding sources and, possibly, the use of direct mailing to members of liberal groups, can provide a base of people who are strong supporters of multiracial housing. Such persons are likely to spread the word through friends, with the result that years later, resale and rerentals will be aided by the general awareness that your community is an outstanding one where people can live their beliefs.

Advertisements in daily newspapers, especially in the real-estate sections, can bring customers. The report forms used at your model homes should ask how each visitor heard of your community so that you can revise your use of the advertising media, depending on whether the desired racial mixture does, or does not, result from your advertising. For example, if you find you are getting too heavy or too light a portion of a minority market, you revise your advertising procedures by placing advertisements in throw-away newspapers which reach predominantly white suburban areas. In general, however, you will have to experiment to find the best way to further your goals.

In addition to advertisements in the news media, rainproof fiberboard signs nailed to telephone poles—giving name and address of your model home, with arrows indicating the way to it—can help bring people from several miles around. Such signs disappear every now and then, but it pays to replace them to attract the casual passerby to your development.

If you have an unusual community to sell, you might find that ads off the conventional real-estate pages of the daily paper will attract visitors to your model home.

Keep Adding Amenities

Small features can help to keep your development ahead of the competition's: outdoor electrical receptacles and outdoor faucets, good planning for the handling of trash and garbage, and more-than-adequate storage areas are only a few examples.

Socially—and, until recently, also economically—Americans are generally moving upward, and housing should be designed for resalability or rerentability some years hence, if the development is to be maintained as a fine interracial community which continues to attract upwardly mobile people.

From time to time, it is advisable to find out what your competition are presenting and to notice what savings they are making in construction costs and improved techniques of building that might save you money.

As security-consciousness increases, it will pay to install quality locks, such as Schlage, even though costs may be somewhat higher, and to consider personal protection as well as design aspects of security when planning the community.

Merchandising the Job

It is not enough to build well-designed housing at reasonable prices. It is essential to provide attractively furnished models, carefully decorated and color-styled so that the consumer has the best possible opportunity to assess its value.

Viewers should see a kitchen with real or simulated food—bread, fruit, cheese, and a bottle of wine. Bedrooms should show off colorful curtains and spreads; toys and books add reality and warmth.

The living room should look as though real people live there; the antiseptic look is to be avoided. Your furniture should demonstrate how two children can share a room. And remember that empty rooms always appear smaller than furnished ones.

It will pay to use a color stylist and an interior decorator. The color stylist is to advise on exterior as well as interior colors, while the interior decorator should be consulted long before the plans are completed so that adjustments in design can be allowed for—if, for instance, the fenestration needs changing to provide adequate space for furniture in a bedroom.

Arrangements should be made for the regular cleaning of the model house or apartment, and the sales person on duty should be held responsible for seeing that the model is swept and dusted, and neat at all times, even if the cleaning person fails to appear. It is imperative to keep the community clean and attractive, and a generous number of trash receptacles will help.

An example of how not to proceed was a large FHA 236 housing development which I visited not so long ago. This community, situated about one mile from a major university and close to some other important institutions, was located in an area with a substantial black population, yet sufficiently removed from black ghettos to become its own community and appeal to the entire market. This opportunity had been lost: The developers hired a black real-estate broker with no experience in, or apparent concern with, developing multiracial communities. The model, which was open for inspection only from 6 to 8 P.M. weekdays and a few hours on Saturdays, displayed dirty rooms and boarded-up windows, and the inexperienced staff person who showed me the model had no sales literature of any kind. Visitors were informed that applications were available only at the real-estate office, whose office hours seemed unknown.

The guest book is an extremely important way to keep track of traffic. Buy a printed guest book and ask all visitors to the model home to sign. Add "please print" below the name, phone number, occupation, and "how you heard of us." Most people will fill out the items asked. Should a visitor fail to do so, the tendency is for the next visitor to do the same. This can be rectified if a member of the staff prints his name legibly and fills in the rest of the columns after an improper entry. The next signer will then do the same. Residents or friends or investors may have supported an applicant's request for a home. Salespeople or managers should be urged to probe for the names of the persons or agencies recommending applicants.

Records should be kept of the ethnic origins of people who come to see the building, so that the developer knows what is happening and whether he is getting adequate demand across the ethnic board. The headings on his own report forms should indicate black, white, Spanish-surname, and others. (Most Spanish-surname families consider themselves white, and resent being included in a nonwhite category.) In some areas, "others" might well include a heavy proportion of orientals or Asians who, in some cities, constitute an important part of the market.

When discussing sales, the staff should never base its work on the percentages of white applicants only. Ethnic demand can be correctly calculated and understood only by keeping records of the number of whites (or Anglos in the Southwest), blacks, Spanish-speaking, and other minorities who visit the model or the office or apply for homes.

Management and Community Relations

It is advisable for the manager and staff to establish warm contacts with both adults and children. From time to time, the developer-owner should make walking tours, chatting with residents and potential customers to understand why people like or dislike the community. If the model fails to meet the test of the market, he should change it quickly to provide what the market demands. If he is selling three-bedroom houses and finds that there is a substantial market for four-bedroom houses, he would do well to add a well-planned four-bedroom model rather than ignore the demand or remodel the three-bedroom house.

No matter how excellent its managers, the developer should

visit the community often and inspect it carefully. Relaxing with the residents helps to assure them that he is not the horrible, supposedly wealthy, landlord they might otherwise hear about, but rather a representative of an owning group which does have serious social concerns. This should also be made clear through newsletters. The developer should visit the community as often as possible and share with the manager whatever compliments or complaints he receives from the people who live there.

The Quota System and the Prevention of Uniracial Neighborhoods

Although the tendency of ethnic groups to live among their own people has often led to voluntary segregation, the segregation of black Americans in urban ghettos has been involuntary because of their systematic downgrading by whites as well as by their subsequent inability to compete economically for better and more expensive living quarters.

We have observed that for generations the American housing industry has had a zero quota for nonwhites for virtually all new and decent housing. Only rarely was a community ever planned to include nonwhites. We have noted that such restrictions still cover the overwhelming bulk of the housing market: the average American developer, despite the law, is trying to keep minorities in his community as close to zero percent as possible.

Point systems have been used in various areas, to keep out not only blacks but also other minorities. For example, in Grosse Point, Michigan, the affluent Detroit suburb, real-estate brokers developed an elaborate point system, in which a white Anglo-Saxon Protestant got a better score than a person who was foreign-born, Catholic, Polish, Jewish, or black.

Real-estate salesmen have been known to jump over fences, hide in closets, quote false prices, (higher ones to blacks than to whites), and develop phony waiting lists to avoid doing business with a member of a minority group.

However, after the first minority family moves into a com-munity and the real-estate people and residents see that they have neither horns nor tails, no cars up on blocks, and a house that is well kept or even better kept than most other families', the neigh-borhood's opposition to minority move-ins drops substantially, provided that no blockbusting effort is being mounted by real-estate brokers.

The 1971 National Neighbors convention at Oberlin College, after hearing a report on the myriad techniques used by brokers and apartment-house managers to keep blacks out of white areas, warmly accepted the recommendations of their legal panel, which were summarized by an attorney as "Sue the bastards." The gen-eral feeling was that there was adequate legislation on the books to open up more housing, that lawsuits can be filed and damages and attorneys fees claimed under the 1968 Fair Housing Law. The group agreed on the value of such suits for demonstrating that racial steering is illegal because it is discriminatory; they also recommended that efforts be made to get blacks and whites to join together in lawsuits, if possible avoiding volunteer lawyers.

One of the major results of keeping a substantial portion of the black and minority population out of white neighborhoods is the creation of uniracial areas or ghettos. This, in turn, stimulates the channeling of heavy minority demand into the few areas in any metropolis where minority families are really welcome, and, in this way, once-open communities may acquire a heavy minority status. To counteract this trend, quotas have been used by some builders, including myself, especially before the Fair Housing Laws were passed. Today, some builders and apartment-house owners may secretly use a benign quota in order to include blacks in the housing market without running the risk of turning their community into an all-minority area. I am convinced, however, that thoughtful developers who select sites far from ghetto areas can do without quotas if they really want to maintain integration. In addition to site selection, which should supersede all other considerations, the key to achieving this goal lies primarily in knowing the market and working carefully to reach whites, blacks, and other minorities.

In St. Louis, Jerome Berger, a leading manager of integrated housing, summarized his position by declaring, "My quota is tangerine." This meant in practice that he permitted no building to become all white or all black, basing his selectivity of tenants on the attractiveness of the applicant. For example, he would make special attempts to diversify the community by seeking some tenants who were poets or artists, writers or musicians, or sports leaders. As George Schermer commented in *Housing Guide to Equal Opportunity*[7]: "A major factor at LeClede Town was Berger's personality and the intimate attention he gave to every aspect of the operation, including the selection of every tenant."

Berger recruited his families by going to where they were, concentrating his major efforts on university graduate students because he felt they would contribute in many ways to the community while needing low-cost housing. He took great care screening his first few dozen tenants in order to establish and safeguard the character and image of the community. The marketing was done by word of mouth and through a community newspaper, complete with advertising that supported it.

Berger's staff was equally carefully selected: real-estate experts whose prejudices represented the bulk of their profession, were rejected in favor of warm and intelligent people who would treat applicants with courtesy and make visitors feel welcome.

Revels Cayton, manager of St. Francis Square—a San Francisco development built in the heart of a former slum on urban-renewal land—once declared: "If you don't plan integration, it just doesn't work out. A Negro leader told us that if you want to integrate the place, you'd better set up a quota and hold to it."[8] In conformity with this statement, Cayton reserved a certain num-

7. George Schermer, *Housing Guide to Equal Opportunity* (Washington, D.C.: Potomac Institute, 1968).
8. San Francisco *Examiner,* March 20, 1965.

ber of apartments in each building for whites, blacks, and orientals. Thus his buildings had 23 percent black residents, 25 percent oriental, and 52 percent Caucasian residents.

Techniques of creating uniracial communities are used either thoughtlessly or deliberately by both black and white brokers. For example, a black broker assigned to marketing an FHA 236 low-income project in a major eastern city set up his model townhouse in an area to which he had already moved half a dozen black families. When whites visited the model, no effort was made to get their names or phone numbers, and they were told, as were black visitors, that no application forms were available at the model, but only at a distant real-estate office which was believed to be open from 9 to 5 daily. Asked whether this office would be open on Saturdays, she replied, "I don't know." The young woman at the model apartment treated both black and white visitors as if she did not care whether they rented or not. Justifying her lack of interest, she explained that she was not a sales person, that all she had to do was keep the model open. She had no literature to give prospective residents except for the cards of the real-estate firm, and even those were withheld unless a visitor specifically asked for them. At one point, with one white and two black prospects in the model home, she disappeared to lead a friend to a four-bedroom model across the street, while the visitors were free to examine her record book at their leisure. Ten minutes later, without apology for having deserted her prospective customers, she reappeared and answered questions. When a black customer asked her whether any effort was being made to secure white tenants to establish a truly integrated community, she answered simply that anyone could rent.

Both black and white visitors felt they were treated disrespectfully and concluded that this might possibly reflect the attitude of the black broker toward the low-income families who sought 236 housing. The inevitable conclusion presents itself that the merchandising techniques used in the development were extremely effective in discouraging white demand and making this an all-black community. The whites could look elsewhere; blacks had no such luxury.

After carefully analyzing the reasons why whites try to exclude families of lower income from their neighborhoods, Anthony Downs, testifying before the Senate Committee on Equal Educational Opportunity, pointed out that the results of the Coleman Report on Equal Educational Opportunity "seem to indicate a mixing of students from deprived backgrounds with a majority of students from more affluent family backgrounds has a definite positive effect upon the educational achievement of the former."[9] He went on to say that "at least some households from these deprived neighborhoods must be given the opportunity to move into more favorable neighborhoods—that is, neighborhoods dominated by middle-class households of whatever race—in order to experience the kind of environment which will allow them adequate opportunities to achieve their individual potential." He recommends that "each cluster of low-income housing should be small enough so that the children living in it would not dominate the schools which they attend."

Downs concluded, therefore, that it might be necessary to place some upper limit on the number and proportion of low-income residents in a relatively affluent area so that after a desired proportion has been reached, additional low-income families would be denied access or strongly discouraged from entering the neighborhood.

Although I agree with Downs that denial of access is probably unconstitutional, I question his contention that the law needs changing to permit quotas by income. Such laws tend to set dangerous precedents, perpetuating a legality of deliberate exclusion. A socioeconomic balance can be sought and probably be achieved

9. A. Downs, *Residential Segregation by Income and Race—Its Nature, Its Relation to Schools, and Ways to Ameliorate It.* Testimony presented before the Select Committee on Equal Educational Opportunity of the United States Senate, September 1, 1970.

by determining the desired economic mixture as a base for thoughtful planning of a neighborhood.

Generally, the Downs recommendations are excellent, especially those contained in his initial program:

1. Expansion of existing subsidy programs for the creation of new low- and moderate-income housing in suburban areas.

2. Enforcing a requirement that suburban communities receiving federal financial aids . . . put into practice effective programs of creating low- and moderate-income housing.

3. Location of many new low- and moderate-income housing units in suburban areas . . . in relatively small clusters and in individual scatteration. . . .

4. Creation of new educational subsidies, . . . that take the financial penalty out of accepting low-income residents in a community, and convert it to an advantage.

5. Launching of legal attacks on zoning barriers that totally exclude low-income residents from suburban communities.

6. Supporting extensive further research into the practical advantage of spatially mixing middle-income and lower-income households.

It is my position that under no circumstances whatsoever should there be absolute exclusion of anybody. However, when an area is becoming dominated by low-income families, it seems legitimate to suggest to new home seekers that, although they are welcome, it would be wiser for them to consider finding housing in other areas to avoid segregation by income or race. Special efforts should be made to attract people of varied economic ranges as needed. People of modest means and minorities should be scattered throughout the community, using the techniques developed by the Connecticut Housing Investment Fund; the University City Home Rental Trust in University City, Missouri; Housing Opportunities Made Equal (HOME) in Chicago; and Fund for an OPEN Society (OPEN) nationally. OPEN, which James Farmer and I founded in 1975, offers incentive mortgages to minorities and whites for pro-integration housing moves. OPEN's 7.5 percent mortgages save home buyers thousands of dollars. The $20 million mortgage fund, the source of OPEN's low-interest loans, is being established through the sale of 4, 5, and 6 percent $500 debentures and 7 percent $5,000 debentures.

The only solution remains, of course, the opening of the entire housing market to all, regardless of race or class. How this can be achieved will be discussed in a subsequent chapter.

Problems of High Minority Demand in Single-Family Communities

The Shaker Communities Housing Office

The home purchase and rental arrangements described earlier can be effective only if substantial funds are made available to those who actively work for open-occupancy housing. This means that capital should be put to work at a modest return, if the trend toward apartheid in American metropolitan areas is to be reversed. The Shaker Communities Housing Office, located in Shaker Heights near Cleveland, Ohio, has met the problem of high minority demand in single-family communities in an effective and pioneering way.[10] There, the communities have revolving funds to buy houses or provide second mortgages. One of the funds, the Ludlow Company (incorporated in 1961), run by attorney Irwin Barnett, has always paid dividends to its investors and does not have any defaults. Since the Ludlow Company provides secondary financing at .5 percent above the first mortgage, terms far better than those available in the open market, this should encourage whites to buy in the well-integrated blocks and blacks to buy in white areas.[11] The Fund publicly sold $22,000 worth of stock at $100 a share and also loaned the money—$1,000 to $5,000 per family—as short-term second mortgages for white buyers who

10. See Chapter 1, pp. 43–44.

11. In 1974, prices for houses in the Ludlow area ranged from about $23,000 to $70,000, with an average of about $35,000.

were unable to meet high downpayments. It may not be entirely unrealistic to predict that an institution like the Shaker Communities Housing Office, financed by the City of Shaker Heights and the Board of Education (now operating on an approximately $100,000 a year budget, with a staff of one full-time and 14 part-time people), may set a new pattern for American cities, and pioneer an alternative way to busing in their efforts to secure educational integration.

However, maintaining integration in single-family communities is a slightly different proposition, and cannot be achieved without a careful evaluation of conditions in apartment houses. For example, the twelve hundred apartment units along the two streets at the western border of the Ludlow Community were recently integrated and are now significantly interracial, possibly one-third black. Unfortunately, few of the apartment renters are members of the Ludlow Community Association, which has a membership of about 600 families out of possibly 750 families in single- and two-family dwellings and eleven hundred apartment units. Thus the role of the apartment dweller becomes extremely important, and special efforts to maintain integration in the apartments are vital if the community is to keep its interracial status.

The Ludlow Community Association has hired several full-time housing coordinators, paid from funds raised through fund-raising events such as concerts and other entertainment. Some of these housing coordinators were responsible for seeking out houses that were on the market, contacting prospective white purchasers, and arranging for them to inspect these homes. In many respects, the housing coordinators functioned as real-estate brokers, although they did not participate in the final closings. They simply brought buyer and seller together, and let the two parties work out the final arrangements and the sale.

The running of the housing office constituted the major item of the Community Association's budget. In order to defray its costs, especially during the crucial first seven years of the housing program, foundation help was secured.

Several neighboring integrated school districts in Shaker Heights became interested in the techniques of the housing office and solicited help from the Ludlow Community Association for their own housing programs. Thus the Moreland Elementary School District as well as the Lomond Elementary School District set up housing programs on the model of the Ludlow School District and the Ludlow housing program. Personnel from Ludlow were hired to assist the other community associations with establishing their own housing programs. However, when integration turned into an operation that was not only expanding, but also successful, it became clear that the city government's support of housing programs would prove essential. Hence the City of Shaker Heights was asked by the leadership of various community associations to back their integration program, which would eventually encompass the grade-school districts of Ludlow, Moreland, Lomond, and Sussex.

The program resulting from the associations' requests was a joint one between the City of Shaker Heights and the Board of Education. The Board of Education supported it from its inception, while the City of Shaker Heights was initially cool.

In 1967, the City of Shaker Heights and the Board of Education agreed to share the expenses of running the Central Housing Office of Shaker Heights. This arrangement is still in force, one-third of its $100,000 budget from the Board of Education, two-thirds from the city.

At the beginning, the Shaker Communities Housing Office aimed only at encouraging white families to move into integrated areas and did not provide any service to black families interested in housing in Shaker Heights. A year later, the community associations pressed their efforts to get the Housing Office to serve black as well as white clients. Bill Insull, a physician and leader of this movement, coordinated the campaign of the community associations while negotiating with the city and working out plans that would permit blacks to get access to the Shaker Heights housing market. With very little publicity to disrupt the negotiations, the campaign proved successful. As a result, the Housing Office not only made arrangements to show homes to blacks throughout Shaker Heights, but also encouraged them to move into the unintegrated sections. In addition, they were told that if they wanted a home in an integrated area, they were free to use black brokers with full access to such areas, while white brokers would assist them in the unintegrated areas.

The personnel of the Housing Office was chosen largely by the mayor of Shaker Heights and his advisors. The Board of Education assigned its assistant superintendent to work in the Housing Office and act as liaison between the school system and the Housing Office. The program was facilitated by the availability of very able superintendents, the most recent being John Lawson, and an effective Board of Education.

In 1967–68, the Shaker Heights Housing Office directed its attention toward the Moreland School District, which had a high proportion of blacks and contained the area's least expensive and oldest real estate. The community was largely made up of three-family up-and-down dwellings. This area, particularly difficult to sell in the white housing market, did attract some white buyers under the leadership of the first housing coordinator. However, the grade school was about 90 percent black, which led to problems in academic performance and in racial tension as the children moved from grade school to junior high. To meet this problem head on, the School District supported the Housing Office in its effort to integrate the Moreland District. They established a study group from the faculty, which was charged with making recommendations for the handling of the Moreland School crisis. One of their suggestions was the abolition of the Moreland School as a district school, a move to be accompanied by distributing the Moreland Grade School children through busing among the other grade schools. After lengthy discussions, arrangements were made for soliciting the approval of white families to have their children bussed to the Moreland School and of black families to send their children to predominantly white areas. A significant number of families were thus reached and, with the aid of the Ford Foundation, integration was achieved.

The Community Associations' role in the attempts to establish total integration in Shaker Heights cannot be overestimated. In fact, the community associations spearheaded the movement. They are, in the truest sense of the word, democratic volunteer groups which achieve their aims only through the devoted efforts of their members. Bill Insull, discussing the community associations' successes and problems, stressed the importance of never embarking on any negotiations unless a full representation of blacks and whites can be guaranteed. White people may be able to say the right words, but they simply cannot present the intensity of the black viewpoint.

One of the most crucial problems facing community associations is the possible resegregation of apartment houses. This is a risk which may be hard to avoid unless large local and national funds participate in buying some of these houses, so that apartment buildings can be kept integrated with substantial black minorities or even majorities.

The techniques of handling high minority demand at Concord Park and Greenbelt Knoll, discussed earlier, included the use of quotas up to 1958. Today, however, faced with such demand, the building industry is content with taking the stance that their buildings are available to all, instead of practicing affirmative marketing to secure both black and white tenants. Builders thus often claim a lack of knowledge about the percentage of blacks in their buildings. One leading builder, asked whether he would start keeping records on the racial composition of tenants if he discovered that the buildings were becoming 10 percent, 20 percent or more black, said he would do so. The reason such records do not now exist is the virtual absence of black applicants at the average apartment house in a white area.

Many builders and apartment owners today "solve" the problem of high minority demand by deliberately delaying credit applications, or reducing the volume of their advertising to the public. The techniques of exclusion they have devised are so complex and varied that they deserve a book themselves. Some of these techniques are so effective that a young builder, on hearing of the *Jones* v. *Mayer* Supreme Court decision which finally banned all housing discrimination, told me that he felt the industry would not perceptibly change save to be more careful in their handling of phony waiting lists and other means of keeping blacks out. By failing to go vigorously after the entire market, such builders are strengthening segregation in housing, with the consequent strengthening of the school segregation which is its inevitable result.

In spite of all recent legislation, the forces of apartheid seem to be self-generating as our central cities turn increasingly black and our suburbs increasingly white. Fair Housing ordinances—or Supreme Court decisions—without teeth cannot satisfy the rising demand for decent housing in areas that offer job opportunities to skilled or unskilled minority workers as well as to highly specialized and well-educated professionals. The test of any government's ability to deal with the problem of race relations may very well be how high housing stands on its list of priorities.

In the meantime, the example of the Shaker Communities Housing Office demonstrates, on a small scale, that if local authorities and citizens' groups work together, a way can be found to break through the barriers of residential and educational segregation.

3

Techniques for Opening the Housing Market

The crisis of our cities is all-pervasive. In one way or another, it affects everybody: we not only observe its effects but participate as citizens in its drama. Its dual aspects are reflected in the 1970 Census, which confirmed that, despite some movement of blacks to the suburbs, segregated housing patterns had not substantially changed; what did change was the black-white proportion inside the cities. Chicago lost about half a million whites; Detroit, about 345,000; St. Louis, about 165,000; and Newark, about 98,000.

While a dozen of the largest cities had suburban black populations which more than doubled in the 1960s, and another twenty-one cities had black suburban gains of 50 percent or more, these large percentage gains often represented minor increases in the actual number of people, since the number of blacks was so minimal to begin with. Furthermore, the increase in black suburbanites was overshadowed by the higher concentration of blacks in the central cities, from which whites had fled. The following table, supplied by the Bureau of the Census, lists the population changes in some of our major metropolitan areas, inside and outside the central cities in 1960 and 1970:

Abandonment and Disinvestment

Residental abandonment symbolizes the last symptoms of decay, the ultimate ill that affects certain areas of our urban environ-

Population Change Inside and Outside Central Cities, by Race: 1960 to 1970

Standard Metropolitan Statistical Areas by Rank, 1970	White				Negro				Percent of total population	
			Change				Change			
	1970	1960	Number	Percent	1970	1960	Number	Percent	1970	1960
1. New York, N.Y.	9,448,551	9,406,755	41,796	0.4	1,883,292	1,227,625	655,667	53.4	16.3	11.5
Inside central city	6,023,535	6,640,662	-617,127	-9.3	1,666,636	1,087,931	578,705	53.2	21.2	14.0
Outside central city	3,425,016	2,766,093	658,923	23.8	216,656	139,694	76,962	55.1	5.9	4.8
2. Los Angeles-Long Beach, Calif.	6,006,499	5,453,866	552,633	10.1	762,844	461,546	301,298	65.3	10.8	7.6
Inside central cities	2,502,884	2,391,207	111,477	4.7	522,597	344,447	178,150	51.7	16.5	12.2
Outside central cities	3,503,815	3,062,659	441,156	14.4	240,247	117,099	123,148	105.2	6.2	3.6
3. Chicago, Ill.	5,672,570	5,300,912	371,658	7.0	1,230,919	890,154	340,765	38.3	17.6	14.3
Inside central city	2,207,767	2,712,748	-504,981	-18.6	1,102,620	812,637	289,983	35.7	32.7	22.9
Outside central city	3,464,803	2,588,164	876,639	33.9	128,299	77,517	50,782	65.5	3.6	2.9
4. Philadelphia, Pa.-N.J.	3,944,884	3,661,587	283,297	7.7	844,300	671,304	172,996	25.8	17.5	15.5
Inside central city	1,278,717	1,467,479	-188,762	-12.9	653,791	529,240	124,551	23.5	33.6	26.4
Outside central city	2,666,167	2,194,108	472,059	21.5	190,509	142,064	48,445	34.1	6.6	6.1
5. Detroit, Mich.	3,419,720	3,195,372	224,348	7.0	757,083	558,870	198,213	35.5	18.0	14.9
Inside central city	838,877	1,182,970	-344,093	-29.1	660,428	482,223	178,205	37.0	43.7	28.9
Outside central city	2,580,843	2,012,402	568,441	28.2	96,655	76,647	20,008	26.1	3.6	3.7
6. San Francisco-Oakland, Calif.	2,574,802	2,318,802	256,000	11.0	330,107	226,013	104,094	46.1	10.6	8.5
Inside central cities	724,698	874,926	-150,228	-17.2	220,788	158,001	62,787	39.7	20.5	14.3
Outside central cities	1,850,104	1,443,876	406,228	28.1	109,319	68,012	41,307	60.7	5.4	4.4
7. Washington, D.C.-Md.-Va.	2,124,903	1,557,842	567,061	36.4	703,745	495,483	208,262	42.0	24.6	24.0
Inside central city	209,272	345,263	-135,991	-39.4	537,712	411,737	125,975	30.6	71.1	53.9
Outside central city	1,915,631	1,212,579	703,052	58.0	166,033	83,743	82,287	98.3	7.9	6.4
8. Boston, Mass.	2,602,741	2,508,377	94,364	3.8	127,035	77,792	49,243	63.3	4.6	3.0
Inside central city	524,709	628,704	-103,995	-16.5	104,707	63,165	41,542	65.8	16.3	9.1

9. Pittsburgh, Pa.	2,226,021	2,241,910	-16,889	-0.8	169,884	161,499	8,385	5.2	7.1	6.7
Inside central city	412,280	502,593	-90,313	-18.0	104,904	100,692	4,212	4.2	20.2	16.7
Outside central city	1,812,741	1,739,317	73,424	4.2	64,980	60,807	4,173	6.9	3.5	3.4
10. St. Louis, Mo.-Ill.	1,975,145	1,803,239	188,906	9.4	378,816	295,416	83,400	28.2	16.0	14.0
Inside central city	364,992	534,004	-169,012	-31.6	254,191	214,377	39,814	18.6	40.9	28.6
Outside central city	1,610,153	1,272,235	337,918	26.6	124,625	81,039	43,586	53.8	7.2	6.0
11. Baltimore, Md.	1,589,099	1,413,282	155,817	11.0	490,224	385,995	104,229	27.0	23.7	21.4
Inside central city	479,837	610,608	-130,771	-21.4	420,210	325,589	94,621	29.1	46.4	34.7
Outside central city	1,089,262	802,674	286,588	35.7	70,014	60,406	9,608	15.9	6.0	7.0
12. Cleveland, Ohio	1,721,612	1,646,995	74,617	4.5	332,614	258,917	73,697	28.5	16.1	13.6
Inside central city	458,084	622,942	-164,858	-26.5	287,841	250,818	37,023	14.8	38.3	28.6
Outside central city	1,263,528	1,024,053	239,475	23.4	44,773	8,099	36,674	452.8	3.4	0.8
13. Houston, Tex.	1,585,043	1,138,014	448,029	39.4	383,807	277,049	106,758	38.5	19.3	19.5
Inside central city	904,443	720,547	183,896	25.5	316,992	215,037	101,955	47.4	25.7	22.9
Outside central city	681,600	417,467	264,133	63.3	66,815	62,012	4,803	7.7	8.9	12.9
14. Newark, N.J.	1,493,788	1,462,248	31,540	2.2	348,342	224,084	124,258	55.5	18.8	13.3
Inside central city	168,382	265,889	-97,507	-36.7	207,458	138,035	69,423	50.3	54.2	34.1
Outside central city	1,325,406	1,196,359	129,047	10.8	140,884	86,049	54,835	63.7	9.6	6.7
15. Minneapolis-St. Paul, Minn.	1,763,769	1,454,626	309,143	21.3	32,118	20,702	11,416	55.1	1.8	1.4
Inside central cities	702,185	771,372	-69,217	-9.0	29,935	20,025	9,910	49.5	4.0	2.5
Outside central cities	1,061,614	683,254	378,360	55.4	2,183	677	1,506	222.5	0.2	0.1
16. Dallas, Tex.	1,295,014	951,048	343,966	36.2	248,666	165,800	82,866	50.0	15.9	14.8
Inside central cities	626,146	548,473	77,673	14.2	210,342	129,242	81,100	62.8	24.9	19.0
Outside central cities	668,868	402,575	266,293	66.1	38,324	36,558	1,766	4.8	5.2	8.3
17. Seattle-Everett, Wash.	1,336,979	1,054,291	282,688	26.8	41,609	28,261	13,348	47.2	2.9	2.8
Inside central cities	518,324	550,419	-34,095	-6.2	38,248	27,120	11,128	41.0	6.5	4.5
Outside central cities	820,655	503,872	316,783	62.9	3,361	1,141	2,220	194.6	0.4	0.2
18. Anaheim-Santa Ana-Garden Grove, Calif.	1,381,742	694,354	687,388	99.0	10,179	3,171	7,008	221.0	0.7	0.5
Inside central cities	429,221	284,637	144,584	50.8	7,063	1,841	5,222	283.7	1.6	0.6
Outside central cities	952,521	409,717	542,804	132.5	3,116	1,330	1,786	134.3	0.3	0.3

Bureau of the Census, *1970 Census of Population and Housing. General Demographic Trends in Metropolitan Areas, 1960 to 1970. PHC (2)—1* (Washington, D.C.: Bureau of the Census, Oct. 1971), table 10.

ment. It is a gradual process, culminating in a landlord's decision to minimize his expenditures and gradually relinquish all claims to his property; the large-scale result is massive disinvestment of capital from the decaying area. The effect of vacant buildings on the surrounding neighborhood can be devastating. Crime, vandalism, the exodus to the suburbs, taxes, inflation, and the cities' failure to enforce housing codes and maintain services at high levels of performance are only some of the factors that cause a neighborhood to decline and a building to be abandoned. The available evidence suggests that despite our present severe housing shortage, residential abandonment will increase nationally. It is a contagious process which can be halted only by comprehensive programs on a neighborhood scale, programs which not only restore vacant buildings, but also increase the quantity and quality of housing and community services.

In 1960, Jane Werner Watson gave an excellent description of blight in the early stages of abandonment in her story of the Hyde Park-Kenwood Community Conference:

On Chicago's bustling South Side . . . were two attractive suburbs, Kenwood and Hyde Park. They had tree-shaded streets lined with large homes; they had a fine stretch of lake shore, green parks, museums, the stately campus of the University of Chicago, a railway giving rapid service to the downtown area, schools, shops and churches —everything, it seemed, that was needed for pleasant city living.

But as years went by, apartment buildings crowded many of the blocks; some of the old one-family houses were cut up into small housekeeping units on a kitchenette and share-the-bath basis. The area began to show signs of overcrowding and neglect. Still, most of the residents were "white-collar" workers in the middle and upper-middle income brackets.

Then, in the decade between 1940 and 1950, up to Chicago from the rural South streamed 130,000 Negroes—and also many rural poor-whites—seeking more highly-paid industrial jobs in the city. The large Negro section adjoining Hyde Park–Kenwood was soon bursting at its seams.

Negroes began to spread out into Kenwood and Hyde Park, and as they spread, a familiar pattern of decay attacked the neighborhoods.

According to the author, the blight which developed in many northern cities should not be attributed solely to the mass influx of southern blacks, but also to wartime crowding and lack of repairs that made some neighborhoods undesirable places to live in. After the war, those who could moved to the suburbs, while blacks, deprived of locational choice, filled the vacancies.

Watson went on to describe the familiar process of panic and decay which has ruined many neighborhoods:

A few Negroes move into buildings which have been allowed to run down. Real estate speculators start visiting all the home-owners in those blocks, offering to buy their property quickly, "before its value drops out of sight." Some of them sell hastily; unscrupulous real estate men then resell the property to more Negroes at very high prices because the Negroes . . . must live where they can.

If the property is an apartment house, the speculator who decides to rent to Negroes may raise all the rents drastically. White tenants will move rather than pay unfair rents, for they have no trouble finding other quarters. This is harder for Negro families so they stay and pay. If the rents prove more than they can manage, they take in another family to share the apartment or rent out rooms, causing overcrowding. At the same time, the owners cut down on maintenance, feeling non-white tenants do not need good service. So the buildings and the blocks deteriorate into slums.[1]

The author then described how the remaining white residents, along with their new black neighbors—who had bought homes in Hyde Park to get their families away from a segregated slum—formed local organizations with block leaders. The result was the interracial Hyde Park–Kenwood Community Conference, with a paid staff which developed a serious urban renewal program.

Disinvestment

The belief by most apartment-house owners that integration spells ruin furthers the process known as disinvestment. The first phase of the process may start with a few Spanish-speaking or black families moving into a building in a previously white neighborhood.

1. Jane Werner Watson, *The Sciences of Mankind* (New York: Golden Press, 1960), p. 105. Quoted by permission of Jane Werner Watson.

This, in turn, leads the owner to assume that his building is going to become heavily Puerto Rican, black, or both. Because he assumes that it will be virtually impossible to sell or refinance the building, he therefore stops spending money on it, convinced that there is no point in throwing good money after bad. Save for the most essential repairs, rehabilitation ceases. It is a self-fulfilling prophecy: gradually, the building sinks toward slum status and can no longer attract the best tenants. Landlords by the thousands have abandoned buildings in many parts of the country by walking away from them as the income from rundown buildings fails to exceed expenses. To recoup some of their investment, if not all of it, owners stop paying taxes for years—for as long as four years, in New York City—before the city takes over the property. Usually, the owner abandons the property at a point when a major repair, such as a new boiler, is needed. The tenants are left to their own devices, and the building is gradually emptied, inhabited only by an occasional drifter or a drug addict. Often fires occur, and eventually some of the buildings are torn down. Others remain; gaunt, stark, abandoned hulks with gaping holes where windows once were, looking much like wartime bombed buildings in Europe. A few, however, remain occupied, and residents receive city emergency repair services.

It is estimated that a billion dollars' worth of sound structures, many of them apartment houses built in the last thirty years, are being abandoned each year in New York City—that is, faster than housing is being built to replace them. In Washington, D.C., abandonment strikes buildings only fifteen or twenty years old.

The National Survey of Housing Abandonment, a study presented in 1971 by the National Urban League and the Center for Community Change, reported that "The oldest neighborhoods and the worst housing" are the most affected by the abandonment process. "However, the process is no respecter of neighborhood boundaries or of good housing within affected older neighborhoods." The Survey showed that "the process [can] quickly spread from older dilapidated sections to areas in which the housing would be considered quite sound and worth the cost of modernization in more stable neighborhood circumstances."

The study identified six major steps that lead to abandonment. First, there is a decline in the socioeconomic status of the neighborhood as middle-class whites leave. This is followed by racial or ethnic change in the neighborhood as newcomers find expansion space.

A period of property speculation then takes place, during which there is exploitation of the newcomers in terms of overcrowding, decreased maintenance, and increased rents and sale prices. The profit-taking at this stage is intense but short-lived.

The fourth step sees a weakening of the market conditions as real-estate can no longer be sold or re-financed at competitive rates, and deterioration spirals as maintenance decreases.

The tempo of the flight from the neighborhood increases, first by investors and then by the socially mobile, until only the poor, the aged, and the severely deprived remain to constitute what the Survey described as a "crisis ghetto."

In this situation, not only are almost all the residents poor and largely members of minority groups, but the area is one in which individual and family incomes are declining while the indices of social pathology—crime and drug addiction—are rising, as are the percentages of families on welfare. "Rent collection and maintenance is sporadic, and real property has become of little interest to the residents and of slight value to the owners."

The next step sees capital withdrawn from the area as mortgage-lending institutions fail to refinance buildings for purposes of modernization or sale, or loan money only for very short periods of time, and property owners cease the expenditure of funds for any purpose.

According to the report, evidence of the abandonment process becomes visible in a neighborhood when between 3 and 6 percent of the buildings are finally abandoned.

When a neighborhood reaches this "tipping point," the investment psychology probably becomes so severely depressed as to preclude any reversal of the abandonment process without unusual public or other external intervention. . . .

The survey [of the housing abandonment problem] has produced extensive evidence that entire neighborhoods housing hundreds of thousands of central city dwellers are in advanced stages of being abandoned by their owners.

The recommendations offered by the National Urban League and the Center for Community Change did not by themselves constitute a program of action, but they did suggest the types and levels of policies that would be required to meet the housing crisis in urban areas. Among their recommendations were:

"Strong immediate measures . . . to suspend further disinvestment in those communities in which the abandonment process is in an advanced stage," including a temporary moratorium on mortgage foreclosures.

"Vigorous public intervention in the central city mortgage and improvement loan market . . . to ensure that adequate investment funds are available at interest rates which encourage proper maintenance, needed rehabilitation and new construction. Such intervention could take the form of direct public loans or government-insured private loans at a subsidized interest rate."

Support and subsidization by federal, state, and local governments of "efforts to test the feasibility of new forms of ownership of central city housing, including cooperatives, condominia, ownership by community organizations, and ownership by public agencies.

"Property taxes in the central city should be reduced and restructured in order to decrease the burden of those taxes on central city properties and to increase the investment attractiveness of those properties."

While these recommendations would, no doubt, arrest or reverse the process of abandonment, they do not offer sufficiently wide remedies for the solution of the urban crisis that faces us today. The program advanced by the Suburban Action Institute, discussed later, is both bolder and more viable. It proposes the opening of the suburban rings around our cities, so that a sharp decrease in the density of their core areas will permit substantial demolition and new construction.

Group Techniques, Urban and Suburban

Joseph Battle's Operation Equality in Cleveland

A major job of opening the entire housing market was done in Cleveland, Ohio, by the Urban League's Operation Equality (OE) program under the leadership of Joseph Battle, with funds from the Ford Foundation, the Greater Cleveland Associated Foundation, and the Cleveland Foundation.

Operation Equality was begun in 1967 with an educational program on the need to break down racial barriers in housing and create equal opportunities for all. It met with little success at first. In 1968, however, after the enactment of the Fair Housing Law and later the U.S. Supreme Court decision in the *Jones* v. *Mayer* case that outlawed all housing discrimination, the program began to change its focus to legal means as a redress for aggrieved clients. In addition, the program included a campaign that aimed at encouraging blacks to seek housing outside the only areas traditionally open to them.

Operation Equality was able to place clients in a good number of buildings by successfully exerting pressure on the management, but the disadvantage of this technique was that its staff had to repeat the same long process for each new success. With this experience, and the enactment of the 1968 legislation, Operation Equality began to encourage some of its clients, who were refused housing on grounds of discrimination, to take their cases to court.

To facilitate matters, the support of the Cleveland Bar Association was secured, chiefly through the efforts of the Committee for Law in Urban Affairs. This committee, part of the nationally funded Lawyers for Civil Rights Program, which operated in Cleveland under the auspices of the Cleveland Bar, was primarily responsible for implementing the Cleveland Bar Association's policy on open housing and recruiting lawyers to handle cases for Operation Equality.

With this backing, OE successfully proceeded against the Associated Estates Corporation, a management company owned by Carl Milstein, a major builder and respected developer in Cleveland. They filed the case for an individual home seeker who had been denied housing by the Corporation, while the Justice Department cited Associated Estates, along with two other firms in the Cleveland area, in a class action. This resulted in Operation Equality's securing from the Associated Estates Corporation an affirmative action program, which included a statement that the company does not discriminate, had not discriminated in the past, and that whatever happened had been a mistake. At the same time, the company decided to restate its aims because it seemed essential for people in general, and home-seekers in particular, to understand the corporation's policy. This declaration was coupled with a directive to the employees leaving no doubt of the firm's nononsense policy: that anyone who violated its nondiscriminatory intent would be subject to reprimand or even dismissal.

In addition to seeking redress in court, Operation Equality requested the Associated Estates Corporation to insert the Equal Opportunity clause in their advertisements and to hire a reviewer for black applicants who had been rejected, to ensure that no applicant had been prejudged or subjected to unfairly stringent credit standards. They also asked that the firm set forth a procedure which would enable them to establish without delay whether there had been a deviation from the normal processing of applications in case of complaints.

As a result, Associated Estates has moved from being a noncompliant agency to one with an affirmative-action policy. This is best illustrated by their dismissal, at the request of Operation Equality, of one of their agents who repeatedly denied blacks access to housing.

The case against Associated Estates was brought to court in 1969. That same year, a compliance agreement was signed. Two years later, some of the all-white units of the approximately 43 complexes totaling four thousand units managed by the Associated Estates Corporation in a dozen suburban areas had been opened to nonwhites. Only two of the firm's housing complexes, one in East Cleveland and the other in Warrensville Heights, have roughly 50 percent black residents. Although the management has been following these buildings with some concern, it has not abandoned its commitment to maintaining integrated housing and continues to market these properties to white prospects. The buildings the firm owns in heavily black areas have enabled them, through skillful advertising, to attract and hold a white clientele.

Operation Equality uses techniques of testing, lawsuits, and negotiations to secure consent agreements with major management firms. In addition, they are engaged in setting up an affirmative-action program to deal with all aspects of the housing problem, including the possibility of white flight and the need to guide whites to buildings that are already well integrated rather than to those which are all white.

Operation Equality has now enlarged its activities by marshaling forces from a broad cross-section of the community in an effort to elevate the open-housing movement to a more encompassing, area-wide operation. This program, the Cuyahoga Plan, resulted in a coalition of members from government, business, the real-estate and housing establishments, civic and service organizations, and equal housing opportunity groups. Its rationale was that fair-housing campaigns have reached a plateau in the drive to eliminate illegal constraints from the housing market, and that the time has come to forge new alliances composed of institutional and traditional fair-housing forces, to unite for the final assault on remaining barriers to open housing.

Operation Equality has been working with the Cleveland Area Board of Realtors (CABOR), who have been responsive to suggestions of implementing the fair housing laws by adopting the National Association of Realtors' (NAR) Code of Equal Opportunity in Housing and creating an Equal Opportunity in Housing Committee of CABOR.

Joseph Battle has served as chairman of that Committee, whose

Board of Trustees has consistently approved proposals for affirmative policies affirmatively administered. These proposals were instrumental in persuading the major dailies and one large suburban
weekly to carry the Equal Housing Opportunity logo and slogan
in their classified sections of the real-estate advertisement pages,
as well as a statement that it was against the papers' policies to
accept ads for real estate in violation of the Fair Housing Act;
pressing for increased enrollment of black brokers in CABOR and
mandated cooperation among all realtors; conducting fair-housing
educational programs; and approving the handling of fair-housing
grievances by the Board. The result of this cooperation has been
the vastly increased effectiveness of Operation Equality, confirming
the validity of Joe Battle's belief in working with formal, organized
agencies of the real-estate industry.

Pattern of Chicago Law Suits

The Leadership Council for Metropolitan Open Communities in
Chicago, formed in 1967 by the area's leading citizens in the wake
of the open-housing marches of Dr. Martin Luther King, Jr., is engaged in a major program to create a single open-housing market
throughout the Chicago metropolitan area. This program involves
action on many fronts, but its priority is legal action. Edward L.
Holmgren, then Executive Director of the Leadership Council,
aptly described the momentous challenge accepted by the Council
when he told the *Chicago Defender* (1970): "We're out to change
the real estate market system, and totally wipe out racial discrimination in housing. Brokers and property owners will keep discriminating until we make it too expensive to continue."[2]

In order to achieve this aim, the Leadership Council takes legal
action to secure enforcement of the existing fair-housing laws in
Chicago area communities. They also work with real-estate brokers, business, industry, and community groups to effect open hous-

2. *Neighbors,* 1, no. 1 (1970): 6.

ing under the law. In 1968, the Council launched the Metropolitan Housing Development Corporation, an affiliated agency which uses housing subsidies to build sound, moderately-priced housing near major suburban job centers. More recently, the Council affiliated with the Home Investments Fund (discussed later in this chapter), initiating a fair-housing service for employees of major corporations. Their combined counseling services represent a considerable force in the general drive toward increased housing opportunities. In 1972, the Leadership Council and the Northeastern Illinois Planning Commission formed the Regional Housing Coalition which, in partnership with suburban mayors, civic groups, and citizens, seeks to expand open housing across a six-county metropolitan area, aiming in particular at a balanced distribution of low- and moderate-priced housing.

It is the Leadership Council's Legal Action Program which spearheads their relentless drive toward equal housing opportunities. "Legal action," the Council states, "was a new tool in 1968, and its efficacy has grown and developed in succeeding years. . . . Each case was a prod to create new precedent and better remedies. . . . Civil rights law is an expanding field, and, particularly in the employment and housing area, litigation has become a significant part of the thrust for equal opportunity."[3]

Since 1968, over two hundred legal cases involving housing discrimination have been brought by the Leadership Council before the federal district court in Chicago. As a result, they have been able to report an 80-percent victory record. Court-approved damages paid to minority clients in 1973 amounted to $54,725, while the sum awarded for attorneys fees totaled $10,090. No other private organization in the country has initiated as many housing bias suits in federal courts.

The Council's dynamic General Counsel, F. Willis Caruso, has

3. Leadership Council for Metropolitan Open Communities, *Guide To Practice Open Housing Law* (Chicago: Leadership Council for Metropolitan Open Communities, 1974), pp. 2, 3.

prepared the *Guide to Practice Open Housing Under Law*. This pamphlet concisely presents the elements of lawsuits and basic forms of procedures which can be used by attorneys in prosecuting cases under the 1866 Civil Rights Act and the 1968 Civil Rights Act. The legal-action program of the Leadership Council, under contract to HUD, has successfully used these acts to effect open housing. Caruso's *Guide* suggests that a white tester, well acquainted with the marital, financial, and family situation of a bona fide buyer who has encountered discrimination, should inquire for the apartment or property sought. He or she should inspect it as though seeking to rent or buy. His application should specify as closely as possible the same facts as those pertaining to the buyer. He should indicate his application is tentative, that he has more property to look at and does *not* yet wish to take the unit; however, he must ascertain that he *could* have the unit if he wished. The *Guide* continues:

As soon as possible after the white tester leaves, the buyer should go to the unit. This brief lapse of time will prevent the Defendant from stating that another person showed up in between. The buyer should make his credentials known. If the buyer is told that the property in question is not available, he should be sure to make note of all the facts. The white tester must then call back and say that he no longer desires the unit. The buyer calls again and asks for the property and again is told it is not available.

The party injured and the tester both should then swear out affidavits relating all pertinent facts to support a Motion for Temporary Restraining Order. This can and should be accomplished within 24 hours, so that the status quo can be maintained and the property will not be lost.

A Temporary Restraining Order is usually allowed in these matters because of the historically recognized specific and irreplaceable nature of real estate. Such an order is further justified by the fact the unit could be lost, because the 1968 Act will protect a good-faith, bona fide person with no knowledge who, subsequent to the act of discrimination, seeks and obtains the housing. For these reasons, an injunction barring disposal of the property in question is vital.[4]

4. F. W. Caruso. *Guide to Practice Open Housing Under Law* (Chicago: Leadership Council for Metropolitan Open Communities, 1972), pp. 5–6. These and the following pages are quoted by permission of F. Willis Caruso.

At this point, according to the *Guide,* the papers for the case are prepared and filed, including a complaint and Motion for a Temporary Restraining Order. The defendant now asks for time to secure counsel or for counsel to study the facts. Next, the plaintiff must get an assurance from the defendant or his counsel that the housing is still available and will remain so until the Court decides on the Temporary Restraining Order.

Often, the *Guide* points out, the defendant will claim a misunderstanding, stating that he would in fact be glad to show the property. Such claims, according to Caruso, are safe to accept, but not in place of a lawsuit, which can then be put on the regular calendar in an action for damages, even if the housing question has been settled.

It is the Leadership Council's position that an act of discrimination "is a compensable act and is no more excused by subsequent proper behavior than a bank robber is forgiven if he returns the money he has stolen. The Court's pressure to dismiss, especially if an apartment is tendered or a home shown, is considerable. This should be resisted. It is our position that $2,500 should be a minimum amount to be apportioned as attorney's fees and damages."

The Legal Action Program of the Leadership Council enumerates the following goals:

1. The development of the law in regard to cases involving housing discrimination;
2. The development of forms and procedures to be used in such cases so that private attorneys and other organizations may take these cases and handle them promptly and competently;
3. Obtaining judgments including money damages and legal fees, so that private attorneys will be assured that prosecuting such cases can be worthwhile from a monetary standpoint;
4. The development of new ways to effect change in the real estate market. In this regard, a suit has been filed against fourteen brokers in one case for discriminating against one Plaintiff; and suits have been filed against nine brokers in another area where Plaintiffs encountered similar discrimination;
5. The development of cases relating to the exclusion of minority group brokers from certain real estate boards;

6. The examination of possible legal action relating to exclusionary zoning and discriminatory mortgage lending.[5]

The *Guide* in its appendix contains sample blank forms to use in filing suits as well as memoranda opinions and orders signed by federal judges.

Especially significant are orders from two judges which show that, while the Fair Housing Act limits punitive damage to $1,000 since most suits are based on the 1866 Law, 42 U.S.C. Section 1982 as well as the Fair Housing Act, damages under Section 1982 are not limited.

The Suburban Action Institute

Another group engaged in opening the housing market is the Suburban Action Institute, headed by Paul Davidoff. The Institute "is a non-profit foundation supported organization for research and action in the suburbs." It was founded in 1969 to advance the cause of locational choice and "focus public attention on the role of suburbs in solving metropolitan problems of race and poverty." Its goals encompass the opening of the suburbs to low- and moderate-income families, in particular to nonwhite families; the removal of "constraints to the development of low and moderate priced decent housing, near job opportunities, throughout metropolitian America;" and the creation of "new opportunities for linking suburban jobs and unemployed and underemployed residents of central city slums and ghettos." To achieve these goals, the Institute "undertakes programs in housing, employment, land use, and municipal taxation and carries out the research needed to support these programs." Their research activities comprise technical assistance to organizations and community groups; background research for litigation; contract research, such as their *Study of Exclusion* for the Department of Community Affairs of the Com-

5. Caruso, *op. cit.*, pp. 8, 10.

monwealth of Pennsylvania; and independent research which focuses, for instance, on "new forms of land use controls and their effect on the development of low and moderate income housing throughout metropolitan areas."

To increase support for their goal of "an open suburban frontier," the Institute recently expanded its community organization activities in both New Jersey and Connecticut. In New Jersey, their contacts with state government officials, labor, industry, and civil-rights groups as well as with civic and religious organizations revealed a remarkable willingness to "pursue the objectives of equitable land use and locational choice."[6] As a result of these contacts, CEASE (the Coalition to End All Suburban Exclusion) in Essex County was set up in 1973. At the organizing meeting, more than fifty New Jersey leaders, including the mayors of East Orange, Orange, and Newark, endorsed the statement of purpose pledging to support CEASE, "a broad-based alliance of citizens and institutions from the public and private sector of Essex County, New Jersey, formed for the purpose of achieving a more socially and economically equitable housing and employment growth policy in Essex County and its environs . . . [employing] all the means of advocacy at its disposal to accomplish this." The Institute expects CEASE to develop as a model, leading to a state-wide coalition of county organizations.

Members of the Institute hold that balanced metropolitan developments, or renewal of core cities, cannot take place as long as local and suburban zoning effectively restrict jobs and housing to the more affluent, white sector of the population. A large number of low- and moderate-income families continues to be zoned out of the suburbs which, today, in many parts of the country, provide more job opportunities than the central cities. The enforcement of restrictive zoning regulations thus perpetuates social

6. Suburban Action, *A Report on 1973 Program Activities* (Tarrytown, N.Y.: Suburban Action, December 1973). Suburban Action, *A Progress Report* (Tarrytown, N.Y.: Suburban Action, July 1, 1974).

and economic segregation and, in turn, institutionalizes busing as a means of establishing equality in education. The scales—as usual —are weighted against minorities and those least able to compete in the "open" market. On the practical level, this situation calls for a broad revision of suburban building and zoning codes as well as of local tax patterns. Such reforms require, of course, the active cooperation of state legislatures and the courts. They also require a willingness on the part of business and industry wishing to relocate in the suburbs to yield, however slowly, to the mandates of law and justice which include corporate responsibility toward their employees, or affirmative actions on their behalf—a recognition, in other words, of making their moves dependent on the availability of low- and moderate-priced, truly open housing for their work force and all the amenities of a decent, pleasant environment.

While fighting exclusionary or restrictive zoning, the Institute supports, however, all efforts, codes, and regulations that preserve or create community facilities in an "inclusionary manner." In those cases where zoning is used as a tool to perpetuate the status quo of discrimination, they believe it to be essential to challenge such codes and practices in the courts. By focusing largely on the suburbs—especially the outer, relatively underdeveloped areas which provide enough space for residential expansion—the Suburban Action Institute intends to draw attention "not away from the central cities, but to a broader landscape that includes the suburbs as part of the solution rather than an enemy camp on the outskirts of the walled-in cities."[7]

A major part of the Institute's activities consists in developing a series of court cases and administrative complaints before public agencies to test the practices of "exclusionary zoning," that is, of zoning for large-lot suburban single-family housing, or zoning which prohibits apartments or involves high building costs. One of the first of such cases, a formal complaint filed by the United

7. J. Aumente, "Domestic Land Reform," *City*, January–February, 1971.

Auto Workers Union in 1971, claimed that zoning laws prevented union members—many of them low-income blacks—from living near their jobs at the Ford plant in Mahwah, New Jersey. This case is still pending.

Paul Davidoff holds that restrictive land-use controls which result in economic and racial discrimination will form "the major area of civil rights litigation" for some time to come. Since the inception of the Institute's legal program in 1971, their attorneys have filed about twenty complaints against corporations with the Federal Equal Employment Opportunity Commission. In 1971, for instance, Suburban Action filed a complaint with the United States Equal Employment Opportunity Commission against the Radio Corporation of America. It charged that RCA's move of one thousand corporate-headquarters–type jobs from New York City and Camden, New Jersey, to a two-acre exclusionary zoned site in New Canaan, Connecticut, "would result in the denial of equal employment opportunity to present and prospective black and Puerto Rican employees, in violation of Title VII of the 1964 Civil Rights Act." This action, brought by the Institute, proved successful. RCA withdrew its application to New Canaan for the rezoning of land in the town and retained its establishments in both New York City and Camden, New Jersey.

Other cases filed by the Institute involve A T & T and General Electric. The Suburban Action Institute charged A T & T with "knowingly planning to develop an employment center in a region of New Jersey [Bernards Township] where zoning controls preclude the development of housing for potential non-white and Spanish-speaking employees," and with failing to apply for a revision of the Township's restrictive residential zoning laws. They called on the Federal Government to prevent A T & T from moving to a location whose "monolithic racial composition and exclusionary zoning laws" would deprive present and future minority employees of work opportunities because of a lack of low- and moderate-income housing in Bernards Township, most of whose land is zoned for one- to three-acre lots. General Electric's decision to move its corporate headquarters from New York City to Fairfield, Connecticut, displayed the same lack of affirmative action, the same failure to examine the zoning and building codes to ascertain whether the new community can and does provide decent low-priced housing for its workers. In a formal request to the Office of Federal Contract Compliance and the United States Equal Employment Opportunity Commission, the Institute called on the federal government "to take all necessary actions, including the cancellation of Government contracts, to prevent GE from denying equal employment opportunity to its black and Spanish-speaking workers as a result of relocation."

The effects on our cities, in particular on city ghettos, of the transfer of large employers to the suburbs are well known by now. Corporate moves, in almost all instances, have resulted in the loss of thousands of good jobs without a parallel decline in the number of job-seeking residents. This suburbanization of business and industrial work opportunities not only reduces the municipal tax base but also diminishes a city's ability to meet the social and educational demands of those who are most dependent on such services. The exodus of jobs and businesses from the inner cities may be an inevitable development. But the absence of work and housing opportunities in suburbia for low- and moderate-income families violates federal laws and is bound to increase the magnitude and complexity of those problems that continue to foster the decay of our inner cities. If this trend is allowed to go unchecked, the resulting intensification of social divisions and economic problems could stretch the fabric of society beyond repair. The legal and research activities undertaken by the Suburban Action Institute constitute a major force and are of vital importance to all those who are attempting to relieve the pressures on our central cities.

On a different front, involving environmental factors, the Institute won a decisive civil-rights decision for the United Farmworkers of Florida Housing Project, Incorporated. The United States Court of Appeals for the Fifth Circuit ruled in April 1974, that the city council of Delray Beach had illegally denied the group's application for water and sewer services for the low-cost housing development they sponsored. The Institute's General Counsel, Richard F. Bellman, hailed the decision of the Court as "a breath of fresh air. . . . The first major indication that the federal courts will continue to invalidate local zoning and planning decisions which exclude minority residents. . . ." This decision, in his words, "reaffirms what we have always believed: the desire to preserve the environment . . . may not serve as a pretext for obstruction of efforts to secure decent and equal housing opportunities for all Americans."

Westchester Residential Opportunities, Incorporated

Westchester Residential Opportunities, Inc. (WRO), a tax-exempt nonprofit organization, was formed in October 1968. Its aim is to expand home-ownership and housing opportunities in Westchester County for members of minority groups, thus reducing the extent of segregated living patterns. WRO has embarked on a program that attempts to transform seemingly firmly established policies and ingrained attitudes by persuading real-estate brokers and homeowners to sell houses on a nondiscriminatory basis; by inducing banks to make mortgages; and by encouraging corporations to assist their minority employees to find homes.

WRO's board is chaired by Kenneth Clark, the psychologist, past president of the Metropolitan Applied Research Center and a member of the New York State Board of Regents. Roger N. Beilenson, now president of the board of directors, was, at the time this was written, its executive vice-president.

While promoting homeownership, WRO also stresses the point that all families—black, white, or Spanish speaking—are free, under law and in fact, to live anywhere they like. Families who seek WRO's assistance are given confidential financial interviews and advice; are referred to over 150 cooperating licensed real-estate brokers; and are aided in combating racial discrimination wherever it should occur. WRO also arranges bank mortgage financing and, in some instances, makes modest second mortgage loans from its own loan fund. All these services are free and form part of WRO's major goal: trying to change the entrenched practices of real-estate brokers, bankers, builders, and corporate employers in order to transform the traditional dual housing market into a single, unified market which serves blacks and whites equally.

In 1973, according to its Annual Report, WRO made or committed second mortgages totaling $58,000 to 10 home buyers "whose moves promoted racial integration in housing." The funds for such loans are raised through a line of credit with a local commercial bank which is guaranteed by individuals and a number of churches. Second mortgage loans, self-amortizing, are made at 7 percent for five years. Since all mortgages have to be fully repayable by June 10, 1978, the first group of guarantors can look forward to a definite termination of their guarantee obligations.[8] WRO is in the process of forming a new pool of guarantors to guarantee a second line of credit from the County Trust Company. Safeguards against loss include:

1. The requirement of a 10-percent downpayment by the home buyer;
2. The second mortgage held by WRO;
3. WRO's $2,000 loan repayment fund (unused);
4. The approval of all second mortgages by WRO's loan committee and the bank making the first mortgage;
5. The deposit of monthly mortgage payments received by WRO in its line-of-credit account, which is charged monthly by the County Trust Company;
6. WRO's willingness to foreclose a house as a last resort.

In addition, all guarantors share any loss *pro rata* under the terms of a sharing agreement. This means that a $10,000 guaran-

8. This and the following information is contained in a memorandum "Summary of WRO Second Mortgage Lending," May 1973, which was made available to the author by WRO.

Airview of Concord Park, Trevose, Bucks County, Pennsylvania. Completed in 1954. Concord Park, a development of three- and four-bedroom ranch homes, was the author's first integrated community.

Integration works! Children at play in Concord Park.

Integration works! A social get-together of neighbors and friends at Concord Park.

Airview of Greenbelt Knoll, the author's second integrated development. The nine-acre wooded site, with its 19 three- and five-bedroom homes, is surrounded by parks on four sides.

One of Greenbelt Knoll's post-and-beam houses designed by architect Robert Bishop of Montgomery & Bishop.

An interior at Greenbelt Knoll, showing the twenty-seven-foot-long glass wall in the living room and the fireplace set into it.

Morris Milgram, President of Modern Community Developers (MCD) and Reverend B. J. Anderson, Chairman of the Executive Committee of MCD, at one of the two integrated communities at Princeton, New Jersey, whose successful sales in 1957 led to the setting up of MCD.

University Heights, Providence, Rhode Island, an integrated garden apartment community organized by Irvin J. Fain, a leading Providence industrialist, and Modern Community Developers.

Another view of University Heights' garden apartment buildings.

Founding dinner of Modern Community Developers (the author's first national company) in May, 1958, at the Savoy Plaza, New York City. Left to right: Marietta Tree, Morris Milgram, Jackie Robinson, Adlai Stevenson, the late Frank Loescher, former director of the Mayor's Commission on Human Relations in Philadelphia, A. Philip Randolph, then President of the Brotherhood of Sleeping Car Porters, and Kivie Kaplan, industrialist, philanthropist, and later President of the NAACP.

Partners in Housing (PH), a socially oriented limited partnership providing tax shelter for its investors, was founded by the author in 1969 to develop and strengthen multiracial housing. Today, PH has varying percentage interests in eight completed developments in Massachusetts, Virginia, Texas, and California. In Brookside, a 375-unit Planned Residential Development (Newtown, Bucks County, Pennsylvania) now under construction, PH has a 99 percent interest. The following photographs (11–20) show some of these developments.

Rockland Place, Rockland, Massachusetts, consists of 202 one-, two-, and three-bedroom units for low- and moderate-income families. Its amenities include a swimming pool and a large community building.

Edwin D. Abrams of Boston is the developer of CAST I (Cambridge Association of Spanish-Speaking Tenants) which consists of 42 units in three walk-up buildings. This development is adjacent to CAST II (not shown here) in which PH holds a 95 percent interest.

Frederick Place, 202 units, in three-story walk-up buildings, is PH's development in Fredericksburg, Virginia.

Casa de Manana, 99 units in 13 two-story semi-detached walk-up buildings, is PH's development in Corpus Christi, Texas.

Another view of Casa de Manana, Corpus Christi, Texas.

Aster Park is PH's 95-unit garden apartment development in Sunnyvale, California.

Playground at Aster Park, Sunnyvale, California.

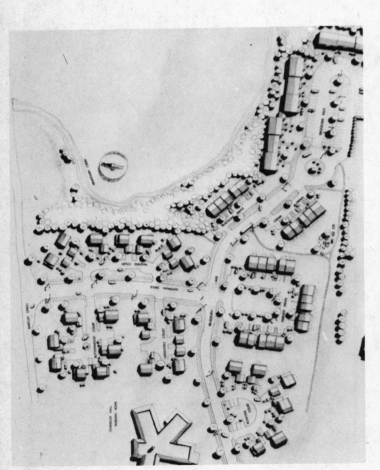

Plan of Brookside, PH's 375-unit Planned Residential Development, at Newtown, Bucks County, Pennsylvania. Top and lower left: clusters of single-family homes. Bottom center and right: clusters of townhouses. Bottom right: apartment buildings.

Traditional, colonial-style, three-bedroom, single-family home at Brookside, New Hope, Bucks County, Pennsylvania.

Row of traditional, colonial-style townhouses (two- and three-bedroom units) at Brookside, Newtown, Bucks County, Pennsylvania.

Black and White together.....

tor, in case of $100,000 guarantees, would be responsible for one-tenth of any loss.

From 1968 to 1973, Westchester Residential Opportunities aided 439 families to buy or rent homes, providing mortgage assistance, extending second mortgage loans, or directing them to brokers through whom they finally bought their homes. Numerous other families received advice and other aid during the same period.

In 1973, WRO secured homes for 139 families, of whom 92 were black, 31 white, 10 Spanish-surnamed, and 3 Oriental, in addition to 3 interracial couples. Their average family income (comprising usually two incomes) was slightly more than $20,000, while house prices ranged from $5,000 to $79,000, with the median price at about $37,000. Purchases included 108 one-family houses, 16 two-family, 3 three- and four-family houses, 5 condominiums, 1 tract of land, and 6 home rentals. Residential integration was thus promoted by 53 moves, that is, blacks moving to white areas and whites to integrated areas; 54 families settled in mixed neighborhoods, thus maintaining the level of integration, although their moves—if most of them were black—might ultimately increase the trend toward resegregation; and 32 families, both black and white, moved to segregated areas, moves that preserved the status quo.

Although equality in housing and job opportunities have at last been guaranteed by law, we have observed that employers, and major corporations in particular, have been slow in making the dramatic turnabout the laws require. Westchester Residential Opportunities has taken up this challenge by extending advice, through consulting services, to major corporations on problems of relocation of minority employees, minority employment policies as they relate to equal opportunity in housing, and on the care to be exercised in selecting sites for new plants and facilities. Under contract to the U.S. Department of Housing and Urban Development, WRO prepared an excellent publication, *Equal Opportunity in Housing: A Manual for Corporate Employers;* HUD has distributed forty thousand copies to America's largest corporations. The *Manual* outlines how corporations can set up minority housing assistance programs and describes how companies with such programs helped their minority employees find homes. Currently, WRO holds contracts with IBM, the New York Telephone Company, Consolidated Edison, and the General Foods Corporation as consultants on minority housing relocation problems, while A T & T Long Lines and Reader's Digest have supported WRO's efforts with contributions.

WRO's operations have been supported by grants from the Ford Foundation, the Rockefeller Brothers Fund, and a number of other foundations, as well as by several hundred Westchester residents, and through contracts with and gifts from corporations. Recently, the Ford Foundation extended another grant which will enable WRO to develop a more comprehensive public-relations program specifically directed at minority communities in New York City and Westchester County.

The Home Investments Fund

The battle for the opening of the suburbs has been joined by the Home Investments Fund (HIF), an Illinois not-for-profit corporation. It was founded in 1968 under the auspices of the Chicago Conference on Religion and Race for the purpose of helping minority families obtain decent housing in the suburbs of Chicago. HIF offers advice and financial assistance on a strictly business basis. It is a self-help program, run by real-estate professionals whose expertise has been harnessed to promoting freedom of choice in housing. Most of HIF's staff is black, as well as its present Chairman of the Board, James O. Webb, a Vice President of Blue Cross–Blue Shield.

HIF, the only metropolitan Chicago agency specializing in information on open housing, enables minority families to purchase or rent homes in suburban communities. Originally, HIF's help consisted of providing downpayment money. Over the years, its function was expanded to include general and financial counseling; referrals to brokers, bankers, and builders; second mortgage loans; information on suburban communities; and introduction to new neighbors. The agency, according to Paul A. Epstein, its Executive Director, offers assistance, not charity. "It facilitates the move [to the suburbs] by putting families in touch with people who have listings and by providing interim financing." The listings are obtained from cooperating brokers who, in Epstein's words, "are learning that in dealing with minorities there are no horrible repercussions."[9]

Families who contact HIF for information on homes in suburban communities have already taken—however cautiously—the first step on the road from the ghetto of Chicago to predominantly white suburbs. Such moves involve, inevitably, far-reaching changes in the lives of HIF's clients, who should be viewed, therefore, as the advance guard in the struggle to raze the walls of prejudice that have kept most suburbs closed to minorities. In order to encourage such front-line efforts, HIF tries not only to inform minorities of their right to fair housing but also to describe to them how minority families, aided by HIF, settled in their new communities without incident. A highlight in this campaign is a ten-minute award-winning documentary film, "Making the Dream Work," which explains HIF's program through interviews with clients who have moved to the suburbs. This film also formed the basis for a number of short television spots that were shown as a public service on all television stations in Chicago. As a result of HIF's publicity campaign, there has been a noticeable greater awareness of open-housing opportunities among Chicago-area residents. In 1972, for example, twelve hundred families called HIF for information. Half the calls were in direct response to the television spot announcements; some 25 percent could be traced back to interview shows or radio and newspaper stories; and an-

9. *Chicago Sun-Times,* October 1, 1970.

other 25 percent were referred to HIF by friends who had used its services, or by other agencies.[10]

HIF's educational program is directed not only toward minority home seekers, but also toward changing the attitudes of brokers, builders, and those in charge of loan institutions. These efforts culminated in the emergence, throughout the metropolitan area of Chicago, of a network of cooperating brokers, builders, and lending institutions who, in compliance with federal legislation, are willing to show, sell, and finance homes to and for minority clients.

The Home Investments Fund also initiated a broker-to-broker referral system. Under this program, city-based realtors can earn a fee by referring minority home seekers to any of a hundred cooperating real-estate agents in the suburbs. Thus, for the first time, both white and black city brokers have an economic incentive to promote minority moves to the suburbs.

In another attempt to effect institutional change, HIF succeeded in persuading all major Chicago dailies as well as a hundred suburban newspapers to display the Equal Housing Opportunity logo and slogan in their real-estate pages. And when federal regulations required savings and loan associations to include the Equal Housing Lender notices in their advertisements, HIF, after monitoring their ads, filed forty complaints with the Federal Home Loan Bank Board against noncomplying Associations. As a result, according to a recent survey, most Chicago-area associations now carry the Equal Housing Lender logo and slogan in their advertisements.

What specifically does HIF do to facilitate the move of minority home-seekers to the suburbs that surround Chicago? Since a considerable number of their clients come from predominantly black neighborhoods, HIF reassures them that the white community

10. In 1974, probably on account of the drop in home sales, HIF received only 1,100 calls. However, an increasingly large percentage of people called because friends or agencies had referred them to HIF. Thus one-third of the callers in 1974 were referred by word of mouth as compared to only 17 percent in 1972.

they wish to join will receive them without hostility. In addition, most clients, never having bought a home before, want to know where and how to find a house they can afford, and how to finance its purchase. HIF handles such questions efficiently and humanely. Over the years, they have acquired the staff and a program which enable them to respond to their clients' problems quickly, simply, and competently. By 1974, for instance, HIF's staff had compiled a profile of 121 suburban communities, which included information on the availability of apartments; the purchase prices of homes; descriptions of schools, recreational facilities, and churches; and information on job opportunities in the area and where to find real-estate listings. They also prepared a list of 175 black and white suburban homeowners (local fair-housing volunteers), who offered to give prospective home-buyers a personal rundown of the community they lived in.

Once a client has decided to buy a home, HIF's staff members, who are all real-estate experts, will advise the family on the best way to finance the purchase. In cases where a purchase meets the demands of federal subsidies, HIF will refer the buyer to the appropriate agency, thus helping to expedite the processing of the loan. In other instances, a conventional mortgage from a cooperating bank, a mortgage company, or a savings and loan association may be a better way of financing a client's home. In practical terms, in 1973, HIF referred many clients to conventional loan institutions and private low-downpayment mortgage programs, making arrangements for conventional mortgages for twenty families. This kind of assistance is vitally important, as we have seen how builders and brokers may use a delay in financing as a pretext for refusing to sell a home to the minority purchaser.

Despite the fact that an increasing number of minority families have incomes which enable them to buy a home in the suburbs, some may still lack sufficient capital for the downpayment required by mortgage institutions. HIF runs a direct loan program, which consists of downpayment loans and interim loans. The downpayment loans are usually one half of the conventional downpayment, secured by second mortgages. These loans are repayable with interest, in monthly installments spread over two to five years. Interim loans, on the other hand, are made to home buyers who are in the process of selling their city property. Such loans are given in amounts up to the purchaser's equity, to be repaid in full when the city property has been sold, usually within 90 to 120 days of the sale. In 1973, HIF extended sixteen downpayments and interim loans. The average loan was $3,380. By 1974, the corresponding figures were fifteen and $2,447 respectively.

With HIF's aid, 122 minority families moved to predominantly white suburbs in 1973, where they were welcomed without opposition. About half these families have one or two children; 40 percent have three to five; and a small number have more than five children. Two-thirds of these new suburbanites came from Chicago; one quarter from an almost all-black section of a Chicago suburb; and less than 10 percent from out of state. Roughly half the families earned $10,000 to $15,999; 32 percent, $16,000 to $20,999; 11 percent had an income of $21,000 to $29,999; and 7 percent earned more than $30,000. About 60 percent of the families derived their income from one salaried or wage-earning person; in 40 percent of the families, both husband and wife went to work. Three-quarters of HIF's client families who moved to the suburbs in 1973, were employed in the city of Chicago; the rest, who worked in the suburbs, were thus brought closer to the place of their employment. Their jobs ranged from administrators, executives, teachers, secretaries, and the skilled trades to lawyers, engineers, salespeople, self-employed businesspeople, and government workers. About 37 percent of the 122 minority families bought homes for $23,000 to $30,999; 50 percent paid $31,000 to $40,999; and 13 percent spent more than $41,000.

Over the years, the services HIF provides have increased considerably. Between 1968 and 1973, 4,400 minority families were counseled by HIF, 328 of whom moved to sixty-seven predominantly white suburban communities. About half a million dollars as second mortgage loans were paid out to 135 families. By 1973

HIF found itself "in a strong capital position with additional loan funds available to client families at very attractive rates." The Capital Fund, used for loans to minority families, consists chiefly of debentures at 5 percent interest. According to HIF's Annual Report for Fiscal Year 1975, "30 foundations, churches, and private citizens hold HIF debentures totaling $289,800. . . . During FY 74 and FY 75 $142,000 of maturing debentures were reinvested for new terms of five years. . . . New and continuing investments are crucial to maintaining our loan capability, since the staggered maturity dates of outstanding debentures give an illusion of a greater loan capability than actually exists. . . . Besides the monies tied up in current loans, funds must be available for possible repayment of debentures during the next two years ($165,300)."[11]

During the same period, half the inquiries received by HIF came from prospective apartment renters, not from home buyers. This shift which reflects changing economic conditions, caused HIF to include in their counseling program more extensive information on suburban apartments and rental agents. While only 10 percent of HIF's clients had rented apartments in 1974, about 40 percent did so in 1975.

HIF's running expenses, such as salaries and rents, are covered by an Administrative Fund, which received two major grants from the Ford Foundation. Ford's second grant was matched dollar for dollar by contributions from Chicago-area foundations and the Zenith Radio Corporation. According to HIF's Annual Report for Fiscal Year 1974, the Fund depends now entirely on local support.

In order to coordinate and strengthen the various fair-housing programs in the Chicago area, HIF affiliated with the Leadership Council for Metropolitan Open Communities which, in turn, is affiliated with the Metropolitan Housing Development Corpora-

---

11. Home Investments Fund, *Annual Report for Fiscal Year 1975 (July 1, 1974 to June 30, 1975)* (Chicago: Home Investments Fund, 1975), p. 27.

tion. In addition, HIF keeps in touch with a number of housing, welfare, and civil-rights agencies, such as the Chicago Urban League, Chicago and DuPage County NAACP, Homes of Private Enterprise, Lawyers Committee for Civil Rights Under Law, National Association of Realtors, suburban human-relations groups, the Federal Housing Administration, and the Equal Opportunity Offices of HUD.

Some of HIF's staff members are active on the Dearborn Real Estate Board's Membership Committee and Women's Council, the Home Builders Association of Chicagoland's Mortgage Banking and Equal Opportunity Committees, and other similar groups. These contacts have enabled HIF to expand its services, which now include a New-Construction Information Center providing literature on more than seventy-six developments throughout the metropolitan area of Chicago. HIF is also cooperating with the Minority Information Referral Center, an employment agency for minority workers chiefly in the northwestern suburbs, where HIF is helping to secure housing for the agency's applicants.

With HIF's assistance, minority families have moved into seventy-four different suburban communities. Brokers and builders —that is, those who are willing to comply with the fair-housing regulations—are cooperating with HIF, as are thirty-one lending institutions which extended first mortgages to families holding second mortgages from HIF.

Testing Techniques

Various groups around the country, including National Neighbors, the National Urban League, and the local affiliates of these groups, have developed techniques of checking and testing to help open the entire housing market. A memorandum of May 1971 on checking and testing methods issued by Operation Equality in Cleveland, observed:

Checking and testing are extremely important methods of verifying and determining the existence and degree of discrimination. The evidence obtained can be used in several ways: (1) to expose to the public that discrimination exists; (2) as a means of pressuring the local housing industry to comply with the law; (3) in actual legal procedures, to enforce compliance with the law.

Evidence derived from testing of discrimination can be presented to local governing bodies, housing suppliers, real estate boards, religious groups, newspapers, organizations, etc. in order to enlist their open support in dealing with the violations and disregard of the law.

Checking and testing involves black and white teams, applying separately for apartments at a specific time, with the only variable between them being color. Any discrepancy in treatment on the part of management can probably be considered as discriminatory. Checkers and testers are an important link in the enforcement of minority rights. Checking and testing is a valid legal technique, and the evidence so gathered is admissible in federal lawsuits. Some people see the use of checkers or testers as devious and immoral. The fact of the matter is that testers and checkers are not misrepresenting themselves at all. Without such procedures, lawlessness rules unchallenged.

In 1971, "Shoppers' Sunday," a National Neighbors program, enlisted black and white volunteers across the country to test practices of city real-estate brokers and apartment-house managers in uniform fashion. The project revealed some significant trends. For example, in Hartford, Connecticut, one of the largest real-estate firms had given up the integrated neighborhood as a place for its real-estate transactions with whites. In two cases, the firm doing the largest business in that area was actively discouraging white families from buying there. Meanwhile, black real-estate brokers, in the typical division of business under the status quo, were steering blacks to the integrated areas. In Oklahoma City, Oklahoma, white testers found that houses were offered to them for $24,500 and a downpayment of 10 percent, while the same property was quoted to blacks at $25,900 with a 20 percent downpayment. A similar discrepancy appeared when a white couple looked at another house for $92,000, which was raised to $115,000 for blacks. Another test case revealed that whites in Baltimore, Maryland, who had specifically asked for housing in integrated neighborhoods, were shown three all-white communities, while a black party was immediately directed to the integrated area and given service.

In Sunnyvale, a San Francisco suburb with a population of

102,000, of which 2,500 lived in apartments, testing showed that 54.5 percent of the apartment developments practiced racial discrimination. In the opinion of the real-estate broker who reported on the test, about 90 percent of the developments in the area were actively discriminating. In the 5,455 units audited in depth, 48.7 percent of the managers told black auditors that all apartments were rented, when, in fact, units were available to white auditors. In 18.1 percent of the test cases, higher rents were quoted to blacks than to whites, and 16 percent of the black testers were given later occupancy dates than their white counterparts. In 7 percent of the audited housing, an extremely dirty unit was shown to blacks as the only one available, while whites were shown clean units; in 7 percent, a seven-day credit check was demanded from blacks, while all such requirements were waived for white auditors. In 1.5 percent of the cases, the manager's door was closed to black auditors, but was always open for white ones. In .9 percent of all tested units, there was a substantially higher nonrefundable cleaning deposit for blacks, and in .7 percent a black auditor was required to agree to a year's lease.

This information was secured by thirty-eight volunteers, who audited 75 percent of the twenty-unit and larger buildings. Each building was audited at least four times by four different teams, organized by the Mid-Peninsula Citizens for Fair Housing. This organization is now funded in part by contracts with the cities of Palo Alto and Menlo Park.

With minor variations, the pattern of discrimination is still repeated in city after city, all over the country. Whether exclusion is practiced by quoting higher rents and prices to black than to white home-seekers, or through negative selling techniques—for example, referring to fictitious problems about a property in question—the result is the same: an illegal denial of housing to minority applicants.

The preceding survey of group techniques which have made important inroads toward open housing outlines the kind of hard work still to be done. Broad-based attacks on discriminatory zoning and building codes, and a reversal of government indifference to enforcing the federal Fair Housing Law and the Civil Rights Statute of 1866 are two major fronts on which to fight the tide of resegregation. What can individuals do to create the climate in which enforcement becomes a reality?

In 1956 I organized a group of leading Philadelphia citizens, headed by Clarence Pickett, to seek widespread endorsement of the following statement from an article by Frank S. Loescher:

> . . . if I believe that discrimination is wrong, then I shall try not to be a party to discrimination.
> Concretely, I should not take a job in a firm or join a union which discriminates.
> I should not become a member of a church which discriminates.
> I should not join a club which discriminates.
> I should not patronize a business which discriminates.
> I should not buy or rent a home in a neighborhood from which Negroes are barred.[12]

As a result of a direct mail campaign for signatures, about five hundred leading Philadelphians endorsed the statement, which was carried by the press as a declaration of intention for serious consideration by all Philadelphians.

Earlier, after the Detroit riot, I had initiated "A Statement on the Race Relations Crisis" issued to the press in December 1943 by Oswald Garrison Villard, former publisher of the New York *Evening Post* and *The Nation,* bearing the signatures of 317 leaders in education, religion, and labor. This statement urged the elimination of racial segregation in all aspects of American life. Quoting Bishop Francis J. Haas of Detroit on the lack of friction during the riot in that section of Detroit where white and black families lived on the same blocks, the statement declared:

> Discrimination by the dominant white community, not togetherness, has been the almost universal pattern. . . . Frustration of those suf-

12. "A Religious Approach to Discrimination," *Friends Journal* 1 no. 23 (1955).

fering the insult of segregation and discrimination in employment, housing, the armed forces and in political, social, economic and religious life begets hatred and bitterness.

The statement went on to say that the general policy of segregation in much of American life

proves an insurmountable barrier to true happiness or even human decency. It torments the Negro people daily like a dagger which is always in the flesh. At the same time, by setting white against black in the competition for jobs, a fatal handicap is raised to every effort to achieve adequate economic standards and a genuinely democratic existence for the masses in the majority group.

The statement concluded:

If they are to stop fearing and hating each other, Negroes and whites must *know each other*. But how can they know each other so long as segregation fosters ignorance and fear in the people of both races?

A similar appeal was made by Sponsors of Open Housing Investment (SOHI). Formed in 1964 by Congressman Donald Fraser of Minneapolis and me, as the National Committee on Tithing in Investment, SOHI used as a rallying cry a quote from an editorial by Norman Cousins, in the *Saturday Review:*

Not much time is left. The white people of America are going to have to do something dramatic and they have to do it fast. The passage of the civil rights bill is the least, not the most, that is required. The main work has to be done not just by legislation but by enough individual Americans who accept a moral obligation and responsibility in their everyday attitudes and actions. . . . A national tragedy is in the making. If it is to be averted, the eyes and consciences of the nation will have to be opened wide—and soon.[13]

This was circulated to thousands of leading citizens, with a folder entitled "Help Break the Terrible Silence of the Decent." On February 18, 1965, the National Committee on Tithing in

13. May 30, 1964.

Investment placed a full-page advertisement in *The New York Times,* headed: "If you believe in Equal Opportunity in Housing, Speak Up!" It was signed by a distinguished group of religious, cultural, and labor leaders. An accompanying coupon read: "I agree to become a sponsor of the National Committee on Tithing in Investment . . . a proposal based on the idea that one's investments can be an eloquent voice for housing integration."

Hundreds of people became sponsors as a direct result of the advertisement in *The New York Times,* followed by thousands more to whom the ad had been mailed. About 24,000 people actively endorsed the appeal of the National Committee on Tithing in Investment, now Sponsors of Open Housing Investment. And thousands have since put their money to work in small or large ventures in the field of integrated housing, while other sponsors have been aided in their understanding of the importance of selecting financial institutions for their savings and checking accounts, which, in some measure, contribute toward the advancement of equality.

During 1970, Bayard Rustin, Congressman Donald M. Fraser of Minneapolis, and I, under the auspices of SOHI, circulated a new personal housing-action pledge, which read:

Because one-race neighborhoods perpetuate school segregation and grind in the second-class status of minority people, doing irreversible damage to countless lives, I pledge to take personal action to help end housing segregation.

Recognizing that my housing investments are powerful tools for changing housing patterns, I agree
(A) to become a sponsor of SOHI—Sponsors of Open Housing Investment—an educational agency based on the idea that one's funds can be a strong force for creating democracy in housing;
(B) to try to invest a portion of any capital I influence in developing open housing;
(C) that when I change my residence, I will refuse to let myself be used to perpetuate segregation but will make my own choice, and specifically,
　　if white, I will actively seek housing away from areas of white concentration, preferably on a block where some black people

live; if black, I will actively seek housing away from areas of black concentration, preferably on a block where black people do not live."

This pledge was signed by over fifteen hundred citizens, including a majority of the black and white civil-rights leaders in the United States, a majority of the black members of Congress, and both black and white holders of public office.

On September 20, 1970, the pledge appeared as a full-page advertisement in *The New York Times,* headed "Your heart may be in the right place, but are you?" It continued:

Take a look down your block. Is it all white? All black? Take a look at your school. Is it all white? All black? The chances are that, just by living where you are living, you're actually perpetuating segregation. . . .
The solution is open housing. . . .
Unless we have open housing, we have a closed society. And, in a closed society, freedom is just a word.

The pledge concluded with a coupon addressed to Congressman Donald M. Fraser, Chairman of Sponsors of Open Housing Investment, which read:

I want to be a sponsor of SOHI. I pledge to take personal action to end housing segregation by seeking housing away from one-race neighborhoods the next time I move and by trying to invest a portion of any capital I influence in open housing.

The advertisement was reprinted by *The Cooperator,* the organ of the United Housing Foundation, *ADA World,* and the *American Teacher,* the magazine of the American Federation of Teachers, AFL-CIO.

Unfortunately, only a few housing developers or builders have applied to SOHI for assistance, partly because few are yet ready to commit themselves to the kind of affirmative action SOHI considers a prerequisite to putting them in touch with its sponsors.

The Personal Housing Action Pledge provoked many SOHI

sponsors and others to rethink their own approaches to selecting where to live. This proved an exciting challenge for blacks and whites alike. In my own travels to present the SOHI Pledge, I helped to persuade a white Catholic family from southern California, who would normally have selected a white area, to buy a house on an integrated block in Oakland, where they were warmly welcomed. And a black cooperative housing leader in Chicago, who had applied for housing in Lake Meadows, where the problem was finding additional white applicants, not blacks, told me after signing the pledge: "I could have rented an apartment elsewhere in buildings that are essentially all white. It never occurred to me that it made any difference where *I* lived."

4

Multilevel Action for Multiracial Communities

Neighborhood Action

Interracial neighborhood associations began to emerge in 1949, with the development of the Hyde Park–Kenwood Community Conference in the area around the University of Chicago. In those early days, this agency successfully managed to maintain the interracial character of the area by emphasizing the need to combat crowding and deterioration through effective block organizations. Along with diligent efforts to attract whites to the lovely homes in Kenwood, massive efforts by the university and the city urban-renewal program eventually assured the interracial character of the community—at the expense of creating a new ghetto to the south as rising costs forced blacks out of the neighborhood.

In the years that followed, new integrated neighborhood associations began to organize. Some of them, like the West End Community Conference in St. Louis and the Bagley Community Association in Detroit, made serious efforts, but failed. Others that began in the 1950s, such as the Ludlow Community Association in Shaker Heights, West Mt. Airy Neighbors in Philadelphia, and Neighbors, Incorporated in Washington, D.C., continue as active community organizations today.

The 1960s saw a rapid growth in community organizations as the combined rise of the black middle class and the development

138

of the civil-rights movement led to the integration of many attractive middle-class neighborhoods near the inner cities. One of these community groups was Crenshaw Neighbors, started in Los Angeles in 1964 by Jean Gregg (later Jean Gregg Milgram), and others.

From 1956 on, traveling around the country, I addressed some of these groups on the need for open housing, emphasizing the activities of other neighborhood organizations which had formed to maintain it, and urging the formation of a national association. Such a national agency was conceived independently in California by Jean Gregg. After we met in 1968, we persuaded Sponsors of Open Housing Investment to organize it.

With the aid of small foundation grants, SOHI, then known as National Committee on Tithing in Investment, sponsored the Carleton College Conference on Integrated Neighborhoods, which was held in Northfield, Minnesota, on March 27, 1969.

The Conference participants were selected according to the following criteria:

1. That they be active members of organizations working to make integration viable in well-integrated communities;
2. That there be a black and white participant from each community;
3. That all expenses of participants would be paid by the Conference to make sure an individual's financial status would not bar her or him from attending.

The basic purpose of the Conference was to bring together people from well-established interracial communities around the country, to solicit their opinions and advice on the proposed national agency which was to help them on a national level.

Black and white delegates came from a dozen communities, from every part of the country. They elected Joseph Hairston, a Washington, D.C., attorney, president and agreed unanimously that a national organization was needed which would perform such services as developing communication among the groups, giving advice on finances, stimulating group efforts, providing a data bank, maintaining national public relations, doing research, and developing action programs to take on the real-estate industry and to battle racism.

The delegates decided to convene a founding conference the following year. It was held in Dayton, Ohio, in May 1970 and was attended by representatives from thirty-three integrated neighborhood associations in 25 cities. Joseph Battle, Director of the National Urban League's Operation Equality in Cleveland, was selected as president. Altogether there were about a hundred delegates and resource people, staff and visitors—half of them black and half white. The conference, charged with energy, purpose, and excitement, grew into a real community of like-minded people who, as members of National Neighbors, vowed to promote, foster and encourage the values of racially mixed neighborhoods and open communities from which no person would be excluded because of race or class. For its first year, the Conference adopted as its major program "the challenging of agencies which control housing patterns to affirmatively and publicly promote open housing."

Leaving the Conference, where I had served as a resource leader along with Clarence Funnye, James Harvey, Elfriede Hoeber, and George Schermer, I traveled with a black delegate from Philadelphia. When I asked what the most important part of the Conference had been for her, she said: "The recognition of what a prejudiced bitch I was. I came to the Conference hating all white Southerners, and I came away realizing there was no justification for such hate." Meeting with several Southern white conference delegates and working with them for a common purpose had profoundly altered her assumptions.

The second annual conference, held at Oberlin College, drew representatives from thirty-three of National Neighbors' then forty-one affiliates. It was clear from observing the conference that the organization is concerned not only with strengthening interracial communities, but also with trying to make interracial housing work. Since this requires the opening of the entire housing market, interracial neighborhood associations are becoming powerful forces in this drive.

As Jean Gregg Milgram, Executive Director of National Neighbors, put it:

Integration does not automatically follow desegregation because racism goes very deep in this country. Any neighborhood that acquires more than a token percentage of black residents is bound to be faced with fantastic pressures toward resegregation.

These pressures are only partly due to the shortage of good housing for black families, and sometimes this is a very small part of it. Even where there is no substantial black demand, pressures occur. Because blacks have moved in in visible numbers, the area is seen as deteriorating. Applications for zoning changes and zoning variances accelerate and, without opposition, are granted. Dance halls, pool halls, pawn shops are opened. The city selects the area for public housing, institutions for the disabled, dumps, and large vehicle garages. The state plans its freeway through this "deteriorating" area. Realtors become frantically active as they consider the fact that *every* house may come on the market—their advertising goes to black newspapers, white customers are advised to look elsewhere. Schools become "integrated" and then a nightmarish scene as the whites hang on to their positions of privilege—the top-level classes, the honor societies, leading roles in plays and other school programs, the teaching staff, PTA offices—and black resentment begins to be expressed and reacted to with fear and flight.[1]

She urged acceptance of the fact that desegregation brings problems in a racist society, and confrontation with these problems rather than avoidance:

Integrated communities exist, stable, open places where people of every group are living and moving in and participating in their community institutions on levels undetermined by their race. These neighborhoods work. *But they work because people and organizations struggled to make them work.*

This is what National Neighbors is about. Our members are community groups trying to make integration work. They learn from each other, and they hope to encourage others to confront problems rather than to run away—to confront them with education and communication and also with lawsuits and petitions and other techniques found to be effective.

1. "Why National Neighbors?" Confidential Memorandum, May 1970. Also for the following.

If all of us concerned with open housing are successful in creating proximity of black and white in the now-white residential areas, then it will be the job of National Neighbors to try to do what it can to make the results be integration and not new suburban ghettos. That is not an easy job, it is not an inexpensive one, it is not one that will just automatically happen without any special effort—and it is a job no other national group is trying to do.

This is why National Neighbors is needed—and why it exists.

National Neighbors are spreading their message through *Neighbors,* a bimonthly publication on interracial living. Through pamphlets, conferences, and consultations, they have grown into a vigorous organization with eighty-four voting member organizations, dozens of associate member organizations, and hundreds of individuals who joined as associate members to strengthen their work.

In the closing section of a National Neighbors pamphlet, *Maintaining An Integrated Community* (1970), Congressman Donald M. Fraser, Chairman of Sponsors of Open Housing Investment, summarized the importance of a national organization like National Neighbors:

There are hundreds of integrated communities in the United States. Some are planned; some have come about through the movement of minority people seeking better living conditions. Some are very small; others are extremely large. All share an uncertainty about their future.

The old pattern of inevitable transition is no longer a foregone conclusion; permanent stable integration is not yet a certainty. In many communities, residents form neighborhood associations to support racial integration as a viable pattern for their neighborhood.

Newly integrated neighborhoods seek information as they struggle to find their way to a new living pattern. Established groups seek more communication with each other and joint efforts to educate others to the existence, the needs, and the successes of integrated communities. National Neighbors will strive to perform these services.

To make racial discrimination in housing as obsolete as Jim Crow on trains is the goal National Neighbors has set itself. It is a major aspiration which must be realized, as the survival not only of integrated neighborhoods, but of a free society, may well depend on it.

Programs to Change Housing Patterns

In spite of existing strong federal, state, and local laws against racial discrimination in housing, the prevailing pattern of housing continues to be one of separate residential areas for blacks and whites. To an unknown extent, this may be due in part to the same sort of ethnic preferences among minorities that produce other ethnic neighborhoods.

As long as the housing industries continue to make it difficult for blacks to seek housing in white areas and for whites to find housing in racially mixed or black areas, it is impossible to tell what would happen if the market were truly open. Residents of interracial neighborhoods are convinced from their own experience that many whites would choose to live in their communities if they were encouraged to do so. In fact, many have initiated programs to do just that, and have had positive results.

In Hartford, Connecticut, the Blue Hills Civic Association has set up a housing corporation for the purpose of advertising their interracial area to white suburban families. This enterprise was stimulated by the simultaneous move into the neighborhood of seven faculty families from a suburban private school. Feeling that their suburban residence prevented their acting effectively toward the solution of urban problems, they sold their homes near the school to move back into the city. Shortly afterwards, the housing corporation mounted a campaign of posters and newspaper ads, stressing the advantages of in-town living versus long-distance commuting, and it was soon all but overwhelmed with young white families looking for homes.

Similarly, the Nineteenth Ward Community Association in Rochester, New York, embarked on a campaign of advertising the advantages of in-town living. Typical of the Association's light-hearted self-confident approach were flyers they distributed to a long line of stalled commuting automobiles waiting on a hot summer day to cross the bridge to the suburbs: "If you lived in the 19th Ward, you'd be home by now. Think about it."

More typical, perhaps, is the primary role many interracial neighborhood groups have played in setting up and supporting metropolitan open-housing agencies in their cities. Thus the Park Hill Association in Denver and the Windsor Hills Association in Baltimore worked to establish the Metro Denver Fair Housing Center and the Baltimore Neighborhoods, Incorporated, respectively. In Los Angeles, Crenshaw Neighbors, which operates its own licensed nonprofit real-estate agency, has put major emphasis on supporting the Fair Housing Congress of Southern California.

Another approach taken by several community groups at one time or another is direct confrontation with the housing industry, usually the local real-estate board or a particular real-estate company. The Northeast Community Organization (NECO) in Baltimore once staged a mass demonstration outside the home of the executive of the Greater Baltimore Real Estate Board, protesting steering practices. In Chicago, on the other hand, the Organization for a Better Austin picketed the home of a real-estate agent because of his alleged panic-peddling activities in Austin, and when he obtained a court injunction to stop them, they appealed it all the way to the U.S. Supreme Court and won.

National Neighbors delegates, after voting to make the achievement of affirmative support of open housing by housing agencies their primary action goal, carried out the Shoppers' Sunday testing program described earlier. When they found that even the most superficial testing by black and white home-seekers revealed blatant discrimination against blacks, their inevitable conclusion was that fair-housing laws in themselves were simply not succeeding in producing an open-housing market. The enforcement programs of the Department of Housing and Urban Development and the Department of Justice, while generally sincere in their efforts, are not sufficiently funded and staffed to be effective. The need, as National Neighbors sees it, is for strong local programs in every city whose objective is solely to obtain an open market: by exposing violations of the law through a testing and auditing program; through a litigation program; and by means of a program of developing affirmative action by housing companies.

Maintaining an Interracial Community

The pressures toward resegregation of a racially mixed area do not allow a community to remain integrated for long without an active community program to maintain it. The motive for organizing such a group varies: sometimes the group might be simply a natural outgrowth of an exciting community organization that sees certain needs, but more often it will be a response to a serious problem facing all residents, such as blockbusting activities, the redistricting of a school, the closing of a desirable community institution, or the proposal of an undesirable one.

Once a group is formed, it invariably finds itself fighting on a dozen fronts at once—always with insufficient manpower and inadequate funds. Several factors seem to be common to the groups that have been successful: One is the active participation of a nucleus of residents who are willing to give substantial time to the organization, along with at least one person, paid or volunteer, who will operate a communications center for the group, either in a home or at a community-supported office. Another essential factor for success is the organizing of activities that promote a feeling of community and a common cause, activities most effectively developed by a vigorous campaign on issues that involve large numbers of residents. But almost equally important are community social events that give residents a chance to enjoy the benefits of the interracial living they have worked for. Community Halloween parties, picnics, and block parties provide opportunities for rediscovering the basic human reasons for continuing to fight against racism, polarization, and separatism.

There are no magic formulas for maintaining an interracial community. Member groups in National Neighbors have found that, regardless of their wide geographic dispersion, they face surprisingly similar problems. At their annual meetings, they exchange ideas and techniques that have been effective in one or another community. Sometimes these techniques are transferrable; sometimes they are not. But the knowledge that no group is unique, that others are fighting the same problems, and that more groups are forming each year is perhaps the basis for the only approximation to a magic formula—commitment and hope.

Why do community associations in interracial neighborhoods fight so hard in the face of so many pressures and problems? There are undoubtedly as many answers as there are people involved, but at least part of the answer is that many Americans find integrated neighborhoods genuinely better places to live in and bring up children.

Today, no special knowledge or insight is required to recognize that America's racial problems, so long hidden from whites, have finally surfaced, demanding enormous changes in our society. Whites who live in the suburbs are aware now, as they once were totally unaware, that they are part of the problem. Blacks who live in the ghettos know now, to a degree they once did not fully understand, that their children are enormously handicapped by their environment. On the other hand, those who live in interracial communities, both black and white, feel that they are part of the solution. They have the comfort of knowing that in spite of all the problems, or perhaps indeed because of them, their children will grow up far better able to cope with a multiracial world than children who grew up in racial isolation.

This climate of feeling that one is part of the solution of one of the most desperate problems of our age is in itself a stimulating one. Often in an interracial community, during chance meetings of residents, they seem to be saying to each other, "You know, it could be like this everywhere!" This feeling enables members of an integrated community to face the next problem and the next, and to cope with the prophets of separatism and doom. "Integration can work! It works for me" is a powerful stimulus to keep trying when others are giving up.

Living in an interracial area, demonstrating a willingness to interact with people of all kinds, offers an additional advantage: Integrated communities are still unusual, which means people in such communities also tend to be unusual, and thus the community itself is often more interesting and stimulating than others, allowing for a larger variety of social contacts than are found in a uniracial community. People who live in ghettos and suburbs are often in a rut, living their lives from day to identical day. Active people in interracial communities sometimes yearn for a little respite from surprise and crisis, but they never have cause to complain of boredom.

White-Black Balance and Neighborhood Stability

Almost all of us still have distorted perceptions about the number of blacks and whites in any group. Virtually without exception, we tend to misjudge the racial composition of any gathering, seeing a higher percentage of black or white than in fact exists.

During an open house for parents at an elementary school in the Crenshaw area of Los Angeles where racial transition in the school was a source of much concern and comment, my (white) wife walked into her child's classroom, where all the parents were gathered. At a quick glance, she estimated that about two-thirds of the adults present were black. When she actually counted the heads, she was astonished to find that the percentage of blacks and whites in the room was precisely fifty-fifty. After the meeting, she left the school with a black friend, who commented on how relieved she had been to see so many white people with children in that class. My wife asked: "What percentage do you think were white?" And the friend replied: "Oh, two-thirds." Both had erred to exactly the same degree, and both had overestimated the number of people of the other race.

Worse are some of the misconceptions concerning the number of black residents in integrated developments. The following conversation took place on a plane between Tennessee and Washington, where a white fellow passenger told me that her daughter lived in Rosemary Village, in Silver Spring, Maryland (which was then seven percent black[2]).

"Tell me about this community," I asked.

She replied: "Oh, it's predominantly black."

When I asked, "How do you know?" she said, "Well, I visited it."

This woman was under the impression that only thirty or forty families lived at Rosemary, since she had seen only one corner of it. Having watched some black and white children at play, she assumed it was a predominantly black development because a majority of the children appeared to her to be black.

I phoned her daughter on a pretext and, revealing my relation to Rosemary Village, asked her:

"Is Rosemary really predominantly black?"

She replied: "There are a large number of blacks in the buildings."

When asked how many black families there were, she said: "There is at least one black family to every building."

Asking her how many apartments each building had, she replied, "Twelve." (In fact, each building has fourteen apartments.)

She then added: "At any rate, it looks like every black family has six children."

When I asked: "How many children does the black family in your building have?" the reply was, "Three."

One out of fourteen is 7 percent, which is exactly what Rosemary's black population was in 1965. Yet the daughter claimed that the area was heavily black, while her mother thought it predominantly black. Both mother and daughter were passing on these impressions as facts to strangers when, in truth, the development was simply an integrated community.

Such erroneous perceptions, which are at least partly based on fear of a little known racial group, can become self-fulfilling prophecies. Scores of families learned incorrectly that Rosemary

---

2. For more information on Rosemary Village see pp. 69–71.

was then a predominantly black community—information likely to dissuade whites from living there. In addition, the widespread belief that truly integrated living is impossible—that there is a "tipping point" at which integrated communities are bound to move rapidly toward all-minority status—encourages such biased views.

In "The Myth of the Tipping Point,"[3] Niilo E. Koponen demonstrated the nonexistence of a school tipping point—that is, a certain percentage of nonwhite pupils in a previously white school which will precipitate the flight of white residents from the school's attendance area. But it is still widely believed that there is a specific or approximate tipping point in housing—a point at which a neighborhood inevitably must lose its white residents, to be taken over, in due course, by minority groups.

Judging from my own work, I know how difficult it is to persuade new white residents to move into a community where the percentages of blacks approaches a majority status. Nevertheless, I have found no evidence of a specific or approximate tipping point. A substantial portion of the housing industry still seems to believe that once a building has more than one or two percent black residents, this figure will soon rise to about 25 or 30 percent, at which point all-black status is inevitable. This belief, in turn, is used as a rationalization by a considerable number of housing managers to avoid blacks in the market as much as possible, accepting them only where the law or special circumstances leave them no alternatives. The resulting virtually total exclusion of blacks from many communities increases the minority demand on open developments, thus strengthening the "tipping point" theory. One way to counteract the theory and prevent segregation is to channel increasing minority demand into white residential areas by supplying both blacks and whites with information on available housing.

As the market is gradually opened to minority groups, a question

3. *Integrated Education,* August–September 1966.

asked over and over again is: Can a neighborhood which is half black and half white achieve and maintain stability? The answer is yes. If, as has been demonstrated, a neighborhood can remain stable with a 10-percent, 20-percent, or even 30-percent black population, there is no reason why the same cannot be achieved with a 10-percent, 20-percent or even 30-percent white minority in a black area. In practice, however, the low status accorded to blacks in our society increases the difficulties of attaining stability in areas where high minority percentages prevail. Thus a white family moving into a neighborhood with a large minority population may feel a loss of status. Fortunately, this feeling is decreasing as more and more people attach a higher status to living their beliefs in truly open neighborhoods.

Financing

In 1967, TEMPO, General Electric's Center for Advanced Studies, was commissioned by the President's Committee on Urban Housing to investigate the country's current and future housing needs. Following the demographic trends reflected in the U.S. Censuses of 1950 and 1960 (see table below), and evaluating the condition of existing housing units, TEMPO concluded that in order to meet our housing requirements by the end of the decade, the United States must build and rehabilitate twenty-six million houses and apartments. If this target is to be reached, federal housing subsidies and other measures must not only be restored from their current shocking level of virtual nonexistence, but greatly expanded. Given our current economic situation, it is safe to assume that the number of those requiring assistance is likely to increase. Of the six to eight million families who will need such assistance, about 70 percent will be white and about 30 percent will be nonwhite. TEMPO has projected that by 1978 "one in every four nonwhite families will need housing assistance, compared to only one in every 12 white families [while] 18 percent of all urban nonwhite

Population and Household Characteristics
of the United States and Percentages of Selected
Population Classes—1950, 1960, 1966, 1968, 1978

	1950	1960	1966	1968	1978
Population (millions):					
Total	151.3	178.5	194.1	201.8	235.2
White	135.1	158.1	170.8	177.3	204.3
Nonwhite	16.2	20.4	23.3	24.5	30.9
Central City:					
White	45.5	47.5	46.6	46.1	44.9
Nonwhite	6.3	10.3	12.8	13.5	18.8
Households (millions):					
Total	42.9	53.0	58.9	60.9	74.3
White	39.0	47.9	53.0	54.8	66.3
Nonwhite	3.9	5.1	5.9	6.1	8.0
Percentages of U.S. Population:					
Inside SMSA*					
White[1]	59	62	64	64	65
Nonwhite[2]	56	64	68	70	77
Central City:					
White[1]	34	30	27	26	22
Nonwhite[2]	43	51	55	55	61
Nonwhite as percent of					
total Central City	12	18	22	23	30

[* Standard Metropolitan Statistical Area.]
1. Relative to the total United States white population.
2. Relative to the total United States nonwhite population.

Source: GE TEMPO, *United States Housing Needs: 1968–1978.*

families will require some form of housing subsidy, compared to
only about 8 percent of all urban white families."[4]

These figures present a challenge not only to the government,

4. M. R. Levin, *Exploring Urban Problems* (Boston: The Urban Press,
1971), p. 182.

but also to private developers of housing. As the gap between housing costs and the rent-paying capacity of low-income families is widening, a fresh inquiry into the effectiveness of federal subsidies, tax relief, and public financing is vital.

America is leading the world in quality housing—that is, in amenities and space per capita. We also hold a leading position in the relative quantity of housing production. But the United States has invested a lower percentage of its gross national product in housing than the other Western nations, and many of our existing housing programs seem to be aimed more at middle-income families than at those most in need of assistance. While private industry has produced an impressive supply of housing, we have been slow to realize that poor and low-income families can be housed decently only with substantial government subsidies. Thus the national goal of the Housing and Urban Development Act of 1968, which includes the provision of six million subsidized units by 1978, will remain no more than good intentions unless the government acts swiftly to restore and expand federal assistance to the housing industry. The reordering of government priorities seems therefore indispensable as a first step toward revitalizing the housing industries, in addition to easier mortgage financing and tax incentives.

The increasing growth of school and housing integration suggests ways in which American foundations could substantially contribute to the strengthening of our weakened cities. Central to the problem, as I see it, is the fairly widespread belief among housing developers and consumers that integration is nothing but a transitional period between an all-white and an all-black status. To the extent, however, that interracial neighborhoods receive sufficient support from American foundations, the housing industry as well as prospective home-seekers might change some of their discriminatory practices. Specifically, I would recommend that foundations back integrated neighborhood organizations to enable such groups to have adequate staffs, both locally and nationally, in order to strengthen and enlarge their activities. If grants of about $15,000 a year (depending on the rate of inflation) could be extended to each of the most promising 50 interracial neighborhood groups for a period of three years, they could develop programs to improve integrated neighborhoods, thus making them more attractive than the average uniracial communities.

Apart from preparing specific programs and fund-raising strategies, local associations should furnish, for instance, real-estate listings, a service now extended by the Blue Hills Civic Association in Hartford, Connecticut, and the Glenwood Lake Neighborhood Association in New Rochelle, New York. In addition, there is a need to seek out neighborhood associations throughout the country that are cut off from contacts with their fellow-groups elsewhere in order to compile and issue a comprehensive directory of interracial neighborhood organizations.

America's foundations, and notably the Ford Foundation, have made great strides in opening housing through grants to groups like the Housing Opportunities Made Equal in Chicago, the Connecticut Housing Investment Fund, Operation Equality in Cleveland, the Housing Opportunities Center of Metropolitan Washington, and National Neighbors.

But the need remains for a national investment fund which works with local integrated neighborhood groups to operate quickly in the real-estate market buying housing to be affirmatively marketed to strengthen integrated neighborhoods while providing economic returns to investors. By extending sufficient investment capital, the major foundations can enormously aid this work.

A second national fund—possibly organized by insurance companies—should be set up to finance seasoned second mortgages owned by groups who bought them in order to promote integrated housing. Such a fund might be modeled on the Connecticut Housing Investment Fund, which is aided by financing from insurance companies.

The Connecticut Housing Investment Fund, Incorporated

The Connecticut Housing Investment Fund, Incorporated (CHIF), originally formed under the name of Robert Littleton to facilitate the integration of housing in the Greater Hartford area, was reorganized in 1967 to become a nonprofit, 501 (c) (3) state-wide corporation.

By 1976 it had made freedom of choice in housing a reality for over seventeen hundred minority families throughout Connecticut to whom it has rendered direct service, as well as to scores of white families. CHIF has field offices in Stamford, Bridgeport, New Haven, Wilton, and Waterbury, Connecticut, and has a field and central office in Hartford. It has helped to establish several similar organizations in other states.

The primary goal of CHIF is to assist moderate- and middle-income minority families to compete for houses for sale in the suburbs. It also encourages white families to acquire housing in stable, integrated areas of the central city. In addition, CHIF lends money to families for downpayments as second mortgages, helps obtain first-mortgage financing, and provides comprehensive home-buyer counseling and service. Thus, over the years, CHIF has firmly established itself in both the minority and the Connecticut business communities. The ingredients of the Connecticut Housing Investment Fund's success have been:

1. A board which includes civic leaders, civil-rights activists, and business people, all committed to the advancement of equal opportunities for all. Many members of the board represent major lending institutions and other large corporations;
2. A staff that has extensive experience in business, real estate, civil rights, and human relations;
3. The great care taken in qualifying families for loans by checking dependability of income, credit record, assets, and liabilities;
4. Concentration on working in areas within the corporation's expertise—that is, doing one program really well.

Loans made by the Fund secured by second mortgages are for a maximum of 10 years. The average loan was $5,000, with interest, in 1974 at 9.5 percent. With the interest rate remaining the same, the average loan in 1976 was $6,000.

Five major insurance companies have committed themselves to

provide $4.5 million in twelve-year debentures to finance the second-mortgage operation. The agreement with the insurance companies states that the Fund shall maintain a delinquency rate of no higher than 12 percent with no more than 5 percent over 120 days' delinquency.

In addition, arrangements have been made with local banks for short loans to provide downpayment money for home buyers. When $500,000 has been loaned by banks, the insurance companies join the transaction by buying twelve-year debentures, thus replacing the banks. Commercial banks, savings banks, and savings and loan associations have been persuaded that CHIF's housing program of secondary financing makes sense, which has resulted in their continuing to make first mortgages even in today's tight mortgage markets.

Grants from individuals, major foundations, and corporations have defrayed administrative expenses not covered by interest income. However, a new program to develop other regular sources of income is currently being researched to determine the viability of charging fees for some services, and securing contracts with companies that are now receiving service free of charge. Through methods such as these, CHIF hopes to become almost self-sufficient in the near future.

In the early days, when CHIF was known as Robert Littleton, it leased housing to minority families in white neighborhoods and to white families in integrated areas, with an option to buy. This program was phased out with the use of second mortgages, partly to improve the economic operations of the company, and partly to strengthen the trend toward homeownership.

In addition to its ownership program, CHIF is the nonprofit sponsor of a 188-unit, Federal 236 program, cooperative housing development for low- and moderate-income families in the northern sector of Hartford. Construction and occupancy of the spacious and attractive townhouse development was completed in 1974.

Because of its independence of governmental grants or financing, CHIF is one of the few nonprofit housing corporations to survive recent shifts in state and federal policies in Connecticut. It is continually exploring new ways of furthering its program goals of equal opportunities in homeownership.

While strong groups like the Connecticut Housing Investment Fund have been able to negotiate local agreements with insurance companies, there is a great need for expanding this kind of financing on a modest interest-rate basis so that both black and white families will find it economically attractive to seek housing outside traditional areas. For example, if white families in Atlanta could be persuaded to seek homes in transitional neighborhoods, their moves could counteract the real-estate industry's steering efforts, which force neighborhoods into an all-black status. Such moves are more likely to be made if a low-interest-rate mortgage fund were available to finance second mortgages at an interest rate only slightly higher than the first mortgage, with no amortization for the first year or two, in order to give the family a chance to get on its feet after the heavy moving, decorating and furnishing expenditures.

It would also be most desirable, and another step toward easing the housing situation, if large mortgage companies such as those that financed the Connecticut Housing Investment Fund's second mortgage program, would help establish a national program similar to the billion-dollar program of the insurance industry. The initial goal might be 250 million dollars for incentive mortgages at modest rates for pro-integration housing moves.

The federal government could promote the cause of multiracial neighborhoods by awarding contracts to local joint ventures of black and white real-estate firms committed to an affirmative marketing program to enable them to give guidance to servicepeople, veterans, and government employees seeking housing.

The National Corporation for Housing Partnerships

The President's Committee on Urban Housing recommended the adoption of Title IX of the Housing and Urban Development

Act of 1968. Under this Act, the National Corporation for Housing Partnerships and the National Housing Partnership were formed and financed with private capital. This fund is being used as development seed money and for equity investment housing for low- and moderate-income families.

The combined capital of the partnership and other investors furnishes equity used in conjunction with 90 percent government-insured mortgages. It is estimated that the initial partnership capital—that is, $40 million—should produce about $1.6 billion in new or rehabilitated construction.

The stockholders of the National Corporation for Housing Partnerships, who originally had to invest a minimum of $100,000 each, include such diverse groups as the AFL-CIO, and major American banks and corporations, from the AETNA Life Insurance Company to Xerox.

The Corporation serves as the general partner of the National Housing Partnership, the investing arm of the venture. It provides a wide range of services to local housing programs, including the establishment of joint programs with local builders and community groups; the formation of local partnerships; assistance with the development of plans for construction, the preparation of applications for government insurance and subsidies; the arranging of financing; and work where needed to insure the success of the project.

Because a substantial portion of the low-income and moderate-income housing needs of America involve aiding nonwhites, the goals of the Housing Partnership are tremendously important in solving the need for a truly open housing market. Groups planning nonprofit or limited-dividend ventures in this field would be well advised to consult the National Housing Partnership for assistance.

My own company, Partners in Housing, a limited-distribution limited partnership, has found it helpful to embark on a joint venture with the National Housing Partnership, in the field of FHA 236 housing. Here the tax shelter available to investors is of equal interest to my company and to the National Housing Partnership, since both of us have investors who bought limited partnership units and do expect tax shelter. With its original $100,000 minimum investment requirement, the National Housing Partnership attracted mainly corporations, while my own company, with a $1,500 minimum investment requirement, is seeking individuals and smaller companies that were unable to participate in the larger venture.

The National Housing Partnership is willing to invest in any kind of housing that provides for the needs of low- and moderate-income families. Both conventional mortgages and FHA 221 (d) (4) rental housing, with 90-percent loans and no interest subsidy, are of interest to them. In addition, the Partnership is interested in all state assistance programs, provided the housing is for sale or rent to families of low or moderate incomes.

In the case of nonprofit housing ventures, the National Housing Partnership is able to enter into a partnership agreement with a community nonprofit group for establishing a limited-dividend housing company. Under this arrangement, the National Housing Partnership can furnish the seed money and equity capital. The nonprofit group may share in the cash flow and assume the responsibility for local activities such as planning, building, tenant selection, and, if they wish, property management.

We have observed the crucial need for increased government aid in the development of open housing, and the necessity for a detailed program to implement it. The form it might take was outlined in "Recommendations to Promote Racial Integration in Housing," which formed part of a report prepared in 1968 by Roger N. Beilenson and myself for HUD on behalf of the National Commission on Urban Problems, appointed by the President and chaired by former Senator Paul H. Douglas. These previously unpublished recommendations are contained in the Appendix of this book. Some of the recommendations have already been carried out, but most have remained on paper, still to be implemented by specialists charged with drafting federal housing legislation, and by foundations as they seek ways to utilize their funds.

Foundations

A major step toward the imaginative funding of open housing was made by the Ford Foundation in 1968, as outlined in its policy statement "New Options in the Philanthropic Process," adapted from a paper written by Louis Winnick. With this statement, the Ford Foundation authorized an initial allocation of $10 million to program-related investments. In announcing the policy, Foundation President McGeorge Bundy said:

Program-Related Investments will be undertaken on broader grounds than their conventional market promise of income or growth. They should carry a potential for high social yield and a clear relation to the objectives for which we make grants. But we hope that many of them will prove to be financially successful as well.

We do not have nearly enough cash to meet all the demands on our agenda, so the Program-Related Investments should be a way to stretch our limited funds, as well as to attract the funds of others to good projects. . . . [They] will arm the Foundation with a range of options for achieving its objectives—the outright grant at one end, something a shade less than a regular market investment at the other, and in between such devices as guarantees, low-return stock and bond purchases, and even interest-free loans.

In making this break with our tradition, we are frankly hoping to give encouragement to others with similar responsibilities, but we claim no credit for having been first. Some smaller foundations, as well as religious organizations and unions, have already departed from conventional investment rules in the interest of greater social effectiveness. In the commercial world, some corporations and insurance companies have taken a lead in making "soft" investments toward hard social gains. We are proud to be joining this movement. . . . [H]ousing integration has a high Foundation priority, further reinforced by the conclusions of the President's Commission on Civil Disorders. . . . But virtually all of the funds have been directed toward educational, legal, and exhortatory programs. The Foundation was inhibited from supporting one of the most useful of all demonstrations—the actual purchase or rental of housing for integrated occupancy in neighborhoods and communities where such examples could have wide effects.

For example, the work of the Mutual Real Estate Investment Trust (M-REIT) fell squarely within the Foundation's objectives, since it is engaged in a demonstration to prove to mortgage and equity investors that housing integration can be accompanied by financial success. But M-REIT was neither eligible for a grant nor was it the kind of investment that the Foundation's investment office could make on the basis of yield alone. Now the new policy has enabled the Foundation to purchase shares in M-REIT, a total of $1 million. M-REIT is headed by Morris Milgram[5], a developer with long experience in integrating housing.

It is to be hoped that the Ford Foundation's example will launch a flow of substantial funds in the same direction.

In 1968, John Simon of the Taconic Foundation established the Cooperative Assistance Fund. Participating as investment members are the New World Foundation, the Field Foundation, the Norman Foundation, the Ellis L. Phillips Foundation, the Sachem Fund, and the Taconic Foundation. Ford, the New York Foundation, and the Rockefeller Brothers Fund agreed to join as grant contributors.

The Cooperative Assistance Fund (CAF) concentrates on investment projects that the Fund believes will produce institutional change by promoting economic development in poverty areas, and, to a lesser extent, on integrated housing. The Fund welcomes investments from churches, and in time it may become a major resource for socially significant housing developments.

CAF seeks to bridge the gap between those who require financial assistance and the institutions which are able to extend it. Since the need for investment funds cannot be adequately met by the traditional lending institutions and government agencies—both subject to inherent constraints and controls—CAF turned to foundations as a source generally free of such restrictions. The Fund relies chiefly on the investment process rather than on outright grants. Some of their investment criteria are:

1. To encourage the flow and retention of capital and profits in poor and minority communities.
2. To form links between conventional funding sources and those without access to them. This includes using CAF's "front money" to attract other investments and federal guarantees.
3. To seek to obtain economic leverage from the use of its funds

5. The author left M-REIT in 1969 to organize Partners in Housing.

in various ways, such as (a) relating CAF investments to publicly funded undertakings, and (b) making investments on a matching basis to stimulate investments by local foundations, business corporations, and individuals, or to stimulate the provision of in-kind assistance from business firms.

4. To seek to facilitate economic development of, and improvement in, the housing available to urban and rural poverty and minority groups through means as direct as possible. The Fund is not in business to bring about economic development through such "indirect" means as, for example, investing in luxury apartment buildings (which arguably increase the tax base of the central city and thus permit greater municipal activity on behalf of the poor). Similarly, projects which facilitate the assumption of management and ownership positions by poor people are to be preferred to projects which do not have this capacity.

CAF is joined in many of its investments by such conventional institutions as banks, insurance companies, or the Small Business Administration. This policy helps both CAF—whose funds are limited—and the joint investor, who may be prevented by legal restrictions from extending the full required amount (the Small Business Administration's 90-percent guarantee limit is one example). Aside from these practical considerations, CAF's chief endeavor is focused on actively seeking the cooperation of other institutions. A glance at their reports shows their collaborative activities in channeling the investments of both private and public groups to the weaker developing sector of the economy.

While CAF provides financial assistance to a wide range of newly established minority business and communication enterprises, it also serves as "broker" and "counselor" to cooperatives, community-development corporations, and businesses in need of capital and technical aid. A case of particular interest to housing developers involves the litigation efforts by a Chicano group which sought to build low- and moderate-cost housing in Union City, California, on land subject to restrictive zoning. CAF's catalyzing role resulted in a major corporation's providing an $18,000 long-term loan, with repayment contingent on the elimination of the zoning restrictions. The loan enabled the group to hold the site while the restrictions were appealed, and, following a favorable court decision, the land was rezoned, leaving the developer free to begin construction.

Another case involving site re-zoning was the Parkview Heights Townhouse Project, a 210-unit development of low- and moderate-income housing in Black Jack, Missouri. The developer of the project was the Inter-Religious Center for Urban Affairs, Incorporated, sponsored by the Parkview Heights Corporation, an organization composed of three nonprofit United Methodist Church groups in the St. Louis area. Financing included HUD assistance under Section 236 for low- and moderate-cost housing, and preliminary approval was granted by the local FHA. However, the newly incorporated City of Black Jack rezoned the site, banning federally assisted projects. At the suggestion of HUD, the U.S. Department of Justice filed suit against the City of Black Jack, as did the developer, the sponsors, and eight prospective tenants. At this point, CAF stepped in, providing a $19,500 loan with 8 percent interest to enable the sponsors to hold the land while the suits were in litigation. Additional assistance, which provided for land cost, organizational expenses, legal fees, architectural and engineering fees, and other expenses was extended by private sources, the First National Bank of St. Louis, HUD, and the Non-Profit Housing Center of Washington, D.C.

These two cases involving the breaking of restrictive zoning patterns, highlight CAF's role as a leveraging agent in advancing the Fund's goals. This does sometimes produce a project whose "size and significance is far greater than the modest scale of CAF's own investment. . . . Nonetheless, there are examples where CAF's willingness to invest if necessary, was sufficient to bring about the financing of a project wholly with the funds of others."[6]

6. *Cooperative Assistance Fund, The Second Report,* March 1973, p. 7.

Special Programs for Local Banks and Other Institutions

Frequently, innovative approaches to local banks and major businesses have secured loans at less than the going rate for cooperative or low- or moderate-income housing which otherwise would have been unfeasible. This was achieved by groups of banks banding together to provide low-interest funds for public purposes, illustrated by the following examples:

When New York City coop housing developer Alfred Kazin found costs were running too high with FHA-insured mortgages, he was able to persuade the Bowery Savings Bank and others to provide uninsured mortgage funds at a cost lower than FHA. In addition, substantial savings were effected by eliminating the high cost of paperwork and complex regulations pertaining to FHA mortgages, as bids from architects and subcontractors have shown.

In Middletown, Connecticut, five banks advanced a 3-percent construction loan for an integrated cooperative housing development, while four mutual savings banks in Philadelphia gave reduced-rate, sliding-scale FHA mortgages to low-income families —that is, 3 percent for the first two years, 4.75 percent for the next two years, and FHA market rate (the current rate at the time) thereafter.

Banks are not the only institutions that are willing to respond affirmatively to make progress in housing possible. In Connecticut, a group of private individuals provided $70,000 in interest-free loans for a local group engaged in the development of integrated housing. And the National Urban Coalition, through its local affiliates, has often secured modest-interest loans, contributions, or lines of credit from major business corporations around the country to aid low- and moderate-rent housing.

The Mid-Peninsula Coalition Housing Fund of Stanford, California, provides an excellent example of cooperation between business and banks for the sole purpose of sponsoring and developing low- and modest- rental integrated housing. The nonprofit Fund, set up by the Stanford Mid-Peninsula Urban Coalition, which was organized in 1969, was initially financed by a $150,000 grant from the Ford Foundation. This sum was matched by contributions from Varian Associates, a major electronics firm; the Bank of America; Crocker Bank; Wells Fargo Bank; the San Francisco Foundation; and the Van Löben Sels Foundation. In addition, two companies—Hewlett-Packard and Varian Associates —arranged a long-term $180,000 line of credit with an effective interest rate of 3 percent, the difference between this and going rates being a tax-deductible contribution. This line of credit goes up or down, depending on the Fund's need. These programs have enabled the Mid-Peninsula Coalition Housing Fund to develop several superb housing ventures. Under the capable leadership of the late Alan S. Maremont, a lawyer-developer and then Executive Director of the Housing Fund, and Ira D. Hall, Executive Director of the Stanford Mid-Peninsula Urban Coalition, the group provided housing at first on a nonprofit and later on a limited-dividend basis. Its well-designed houses, on beautifully landscaped grounds, built under HUD Section 236, demonstrate how well such programs can work if they are given strong local leadership.

To satisfy the needs of today's home-seekers at a time of rising prices and high mortgage rates, black-led savings banks have been willing to extend mortgages on the best possible terms to whites moving into well-integrated neighborhoods. The same applies, of course, to those white savings associations which have been offering equally attractive terms to blacks moving into high-quality integrated housing. A primary example of this type of service, according to Suburban Fair Housing, Incorporated, the affirmative-marketing real-estate agency, is evident in the activities of the black-led Berean Savings Association of Philadelphia, which has been a leading source of mortgages for black families moving into white areas.

Groups of savings banks have also formed organizations for the purpose of sharing high-risk mortgages, a step which effectively helps to increase the availability of housing for low- and modest-income minority families. One organization of this type is SAMCO, which was founded by thirty-five Northern California savings and loan associations.

Churches

With the possible exception of fraternal orders, American churches are the most segregated institutions in the country. This situation is reflected in their dismal failure to combat discrimination in housing. Nevertheless, the National Council of the Churches of Christ in the U.S.A. has steadily tried to move forward in this field, as was made clear in the following statement on the Churches' Concern for Housing, adopted by the General Board of the National Council of Churches on November 18, 1953:

In the interest of making more and better housing available for minority groups, not only must the housing supply be increased, but ways must be found to facilitate the acquisition of property for the construction of nonsegregated housing and the rehabilitation of housing for nonsegregated use. We appeal to all church members to support every sound and reasonable effort to put an end to the exclusion of any person on account of race, color, creed, or national origin or ancestry from equal opportunity to rent or purchase living accommodations with all available facilities and services at equitable cost in any neighborhood.

We also appeal to church members to support all sound and effective measures for a comprehensive national housing program coordinated by one federal agency, and for the development of well-planned, integrated, and nonsegregated residential neighborhoods.

Later, in 1967, the General Board of the National Council of the Churches of Christ in the U.S.A. adopted a resolution supporting "efforts of Councils of Churches in all states, counties and cities to secure the adoption of open housing legislation; and [encouraging] its member communion to support such efforts toward open occupancy in all communities throughout the nation."

Since the late nineteenth century, according to Charles W. Powers, some churches have refrained from investments in companies producing liquor and tobacco. While the issue of the social consequences of investment policies was raised in the churches in the early 1930s, it was decided at the time not to build existing precedents but rather to seek high returns to secure funds for church programs. My own appeals to church groups, at the time of the Council's 1953 Statement—that they consider investments in FHA-guaranteed mortgages to enable my first integrated housing developments to get off the ground—met with cold receptions.

"The issue remained dormant until the early 1960's when the National Committee on Tithing in Investment (NCTI), with an illustrious membership that included many leading churchmen, raised the issue in clear and convincing terms by proposing that churches, along with other charitable institutions and individuals, invest ten percent of their investment assets in open housing projects."[7]

This proposal was followed, in 1965, by consultation between church leaders and members of the NCTI on investment policies of churches in the United States. Gradually, church after church started adopting resolutions that called for church investment based on social principles.

In 1969, the Unitarian Universalist Association published the first pamphlet written on the subject, which, in addition to the Unitarian Church's internal discussion, included the Reverend Jack Mendelsohn's famous sermon, "One Pocket or Two for Our Cash and Our Convictions." This sermon called attention to the work of the National Committee on Tithing in Investment (now Sponsors of Open Housing Investment), on whose Board Jack Mendelsohn served.

James Forman's 1969 "Black Manifesto," calling for reparations to blacks, placed further pressures on the churches to re-examine their investment policies. (The 1968 General Assembly of the Presbyterian Church had already directed all its boards to set aside 30 percent of their unrestricted funds for higher risk,

---

7. Charles W. Powers, *Social Responsibility and Investment* (Nashville, Tenn.: Abingdon Press, 1971), p. 15.

lower-return investments.) Today, the major denominations, including the Presbyterians, Episcopalians, and others, have task forces working to develop social investment policies. As a result, many churches have begun making investments in socially useful projects. Both national and local churches have invested in various of my companies, as did the Unitarians, the Quakers, and the Ethical Culture Society in my earlier ventures—for example, in Modern Community Developers (later Planned Communities, Incorporated)—with the largest number investing in M-REIT (Mutual Real Estate Investment Trust). The Methodist Board of Pensions invested a quarter million dollars in M-REIT, and some Presbyterian funds, $100,000. Lesser amounts came from other local or national churches, which included Catholic, Unitarian, and Quaker groups. In addition, churches all over the country have begun sponsoring nonprofit housing developments, and some of them, like the American Baptist Home Mission Society, have set up active subsidiaries to work in this field and have been able to report substantial accomplishments.

Those who wish to examine possible roles for churches in developing open housing would do well to study the work of the American Baptist Home Mission Society, headed by James Christison, and its housing agency, the American Baptist Service Corporation, which has developed an impressive quantity of housing on a nonprofit basis and is now investigating the possibilities of working with limited-dividend ventures.

A major portion of the work of churches has gone into improving ghetto conditions rather than into vigorous efforts to change the patterns of housing segregation. This has been true of virtually all the black churches that have been active in the field, and it is also true of a substantial number of the white churches. It is sadly true that years of discrimination have encouraged many to look for ways to immediately relieve suffering at the expense of long-term change. It is impossible to fault the motives of those who choose to act on the first front. However, it is the pattern which must change if the tide is to be reversed.

Schools

When the Board of Education in Shaker Heights, Ohio, joined with its city to promote integration in housing, it provided an important model. The Shaker Heights community recognized that breaking exclusionary housing patterns and affirmatively maintaining extensive interracial neighborhoods is the key to preventing the segregated schools that will otherwise follow. Had this understanding been accepted in the past, hundreds of American communities could have prevented the agonizing conflicts over school busing that confront them today, as well as its enormous expense. Once affirmative action becomes part of our national consciousness, more parents will be perceptive about trends toward resegregation: those who now understand the importance of staying active in Parent-Teachers Associations will also recognize that establishing separate programs for "accelerated" students results in creating virtually segregated classrooms.

For generations students have been leaders in social-action movements and have contributed enormously toward the solution of national problems. In the past, student groups have worked successfully to open racially segregated dormitories and off-campus student housing. When black college students moved during the late 1960s to establish separate dormitories as an expression of their pride and solidarity, the situation took on an ironic perspective. Many prominent black intellectual leaders, veterans of the desegregation struggles of the past, recognized the trend as a move toward resegregation, and two, Robert C. Weaver and Kenneth Clark, resigned from the Board of Trustees of Antioch College in protest. Their resignations were sparked by a young black student leader, Michael Meyers. Although he was beaten several times by black student separatists, he succeeded in getting the Department of Health, Education and Welfare to refuse federal funds to Antioch unless the black dormitories were ended. As a result, black dorms on many, if not most, campuses are a thing of the past today.

Students can also be effective in organizing their campuses for personal housing action of the kind sponsored by SOHI, Sponsors of Open Housing Investment. This would involve the circulation of the SOHI Appeal for ending ghettos by asking people to sign a pledge to seek housing away from one-race neighborhoods when they move, and to invest a portion of any capital they influence in open housing.

Fair Housing Committees

The Housing Opportunities Program of the American Friends Service Committee has been one of the most effective in the country, sparking new ideas in housing and rendering tremendous assistance to my own efforts in the open-housing field. In 1952, after learning the building business, I went to the American Friends Service Committee for advice on how to get started in developing open housing. They correctly dissuaded me from attempting to develop nonprofit coops as I had planned: in their view, I would influence the building industry only if I could show reasonable profits from private enterprise.

In a coalition effort, the National Committee Against Discrimination in Housing (NCDH) was formed in 1950 by representatives of several national organizations deeply concerned with the failure of the battle against the Metropolitan Life Insurance Company's all-white Stuyvesant Town in New York City. Through the years, the Committee has done valuable work in providing volunteer help and conducting campaigns to get White House action against discrimination in housing. It has serviced many fair-housing groups throughout the country and has conducted useful research on the interrelationship of job and housing access. Its publications, including its periodical, *Trends in Housing,* have been valuable tools in the struggle to end housing segregation.

By consistently challenging residential discrimination, NCDH helped to create a climate which cleared the way for the enactment of fair-housing legislation. During the last few years, the Committee has considerably expanded the scope of its activities. In the legal field, for instance, they have an admirable record of challenging exclusionary zoning practices in court, as well as the Nixon Administration's impounding of the housing funds that had been appropriated by Congress. NCDH's field services now include regional housing training programs aimed at providing community leaders in fair housing, planning, real estate, and mortgage-lending with the information and tools they need. These programs, or seminars, focus on the enforcement of state and federal legislation; the promotion of real-estate practices in compliance with the fair-housing law; the development of affirmative marketing and financing of homes to advance racial integration; and the encouraging of employers to locate their enterprises in areas where equal housing and educational opportunities already exist or can be established. NCDH also monitors government agencies and publicizes their failures to enforce the fair-housing laws.

Together with the Department of Housing and Urban Development, NCDH conducted a demonstration project in the San Francisco Metropolitan Area to develop a model of new and improved mechanisms for expanding and strengthening the efforts to open the housing market on a metropolitan-wide basis and, at the same time, provide guidelines for other regions. The findings of this project, which was approved by HUD in 1969 and closed down five years later, were published by NCDH in *Home Free? New Vistas in Regional Housing* (1974). In the same year, NCDH and the Urban Land Institute published *Fair Housing and Exclusionary Land Use,* a resource for lawyers and lay persons on the official devices that undermine the realization of equal-housing opportunities. This report summarizes recent litigation involving restrictive building codes and zoning practices, and discusses the problems of site selection, the use of Federal surplus land, and other relevant questions.

Finally, "as a national resource for local citizen action," the Committee issued a *Handbook for Citizen Fair Housing Advocacy*

Under the Housing and Community Development Act of 1974.
This publication, while mobilizing the "power of informed citizen
action at the local level,"[8] alerts the public to the legality of freedom in locational housing choices. The manual explains the act
and the block-grant application process, tells where to get local
information, and suggests strategies for developing broad-based
community support and ways to deal with abuses.

Currently, NCDH's major thrusts are in litigation on the wider
aspects of exclusionary zoning and the stimulation of "local
coalitions to do the essential advocacy job in the implementation
of the 1974 Housing and Community Development Act." This,
according to Edward L. Holmgren, NCDH's Executive Director,
"involves a strengthening and broadening of the groups which
are generally identified as fair housing organizations. . . . Many
of these organizations have moved beyond the activity of assisting
individual minority families into a . . . program which includes
that feature, but also encompasses advocacy of housing planning,
testing, metropolitan housing allocation systems and other activities."[9]

Local fair-housing committees, estimated to number well over a
thousand throughout the country, have provided valuable assistance to minority home-seekers in securing housing. Unfortunately, some fair-housing leaders still have not understood the
importance of their own housing moves, in particular their rela-
tionship to patterns of segregation; in seeking new homes, their
personal selections of place and residence too often are indis-
tinguishable from the pattern their organizations are struggling
to change. Going to a white broker who, to all intents and purposes, practices exclusionary policies, and buying from him in an
area of *de facto* segregation, fails to enhance the credibility of
those who proclaim quite another standard for their fellow citizens.

---

8. *Handbook for Citizen Fair Housing Advocacy Under the Housing and Community Development Act of 1974.* 1974. Foreword.
9. Private communication, January 30, 1975.

A number of fair-housing committees have organized metropolitan groups with as many as twenty or thirty or more affiliates, some of which have helped to establish housing opportunity centers such as those in Denver and Dallas. There, as in Columbus (Ohio) and in Little Rock (Arkansas), the fair-housing centers have sometimes been funded by foundations, but more frequently by government agencies, including the Office of Economic Opportunity. The support of the latter has not always been free of adverse effects on the goals of committees, as Juliet Saltman, founder and first executive secretary of the Fair Housing Contact Service of Akron, Ohio, relates in *Open Housing as a Social Movement*.[10] When this fair-housing committee received funds from the Office of Economic Opportunity, they found their program shifted from a concern for open housing to a concern for low-income housing. As a result, the Akron Fair Housing Committee declined a second year's funding.

Although housing-opportunity centers have done valuable work, a good deal of increased effectiveness might be generated if more time and effort were spent on educating local residents on the importance of personal housing choices.

10. Juliet Z. Saltman, *Open Housing as a Social Movement* (Lexington, Mass.: Heath Lexington Books, 1971).

5

The Future: Housing for Reality

Coops

The basic principles of cooperatives—established in 1844 in the little village of Rochdale by twenty-eight Lancashire weavers who formed a cooperative society to improve their conditions—include open membership with no restrictions on race, creed, or color. Thus, traditionally, it has been far easier for minority families to get into cooperatives that adhere to the Rochdale principles than into most privately owned housing.

Although the cooperative technique facilitates the affirmative marketing of homes to minority families, it does not necessarily guarantee the maintenance of integrated communities. However, the combination of group homeownership, active membership participation in cooperative affairs on a one-family–one-vote basis, the built-in option to repurchase holdings, and the generally prevailing philosophy of open occupancy and nondiscrimination has led to the stabilization of a considerable number of cooperatives. Once an integrated pattern has been established, it tends to be accepted and carried over into the future, provided that members of a coop are actively involved in community affairs and are determined to demonstrate that multiracial communities work. Communal activities depend, of course, on the pioneering spirit of the group, its sense of community, and the shared goals and collective tasks which give direction and meaning to cooperative ventures. Village Creek in South Norwalk, Connecticut, is one example. Organized on a nonprofit basis by a small group of blacks and whites in 1949, it has been integrated from the start. For the past twenty-three years, this 65-unit coop has maintained a balance of approximately 60 percent white and 40 percent minority families. (Other cooperatives of the large-management type have been integrated for substantial periods of time with an occupancy rate ranging from 10 percent white to 10 percent black.) At Village Creek, members have settled "into an easy-going, half-taken-for-granted Utopia,"[1] but continue to observe and talk freely about the "balance" of the village structure, and are determined to do all they can to restore this balance through community action should the integrated character of their cooperative be impaired. In 1969, for instance, coop members of Village Creek realized that this might happen if a black prospective buyer were to move into an area where nine out of the group's thirteen black families had their homes. Backed by the local NAACP, the black purchaser was urged by the village community corporation to consider three other houses that were on the market at the time. This was a painful move for the cooperative, for it meant practicing "discrimination to prevent segregation." Unexpectedly, the balance was restored by a white family's buying a house from a black family in the same area, which paved the way for the black home-seekers to move into the house of their choice.

The two major forms of housing cooperatives in the United States are the single-ownership "management type" and the "sales type." Single-ownership cooperatives are built around a corporation which has title to buildings—subject to mortgages—with perhaps ten to ten thousand dwelling units; each member family has one voice and one vote in the affairs of the cooperative. These "management type" cooperatives fall into two major subdivisions:

---

1. M. Hancock, "The Annals of Village Creek," *The Fairfield County Courier,* November 20, 1969.

those which more or less follow the Rochdale cooperative principles and provide housing for middle- and moderate-income
families, and those sponsored by real-estate and landlord interests
for primarily high-income families. The "sales type" cooperative—
for example, Village Creek in South Norwalk—includes communities where each family provides its own financing and is a member
of an organization that furnishes at least some community services.

Although some conventionally financed housing cooperatives
use their rules on voting new members in, as a way of keeping out
minority families, many thousands of nonwhite families have been
welcomed and are living in cooperatives, particularly those developed with HUD-assisted mortgages all around the country,
especially in the larger cities, including the Detroit and greater New
York areas, Kansas City, Chicago, Los Angeles, and San Francisco.

The leading sponsor of cooperative housing in New York City
has been the United Housing Foundation, whose president was
Jacob Potofsky of the Amalgamated Clothing Workers of America. The UHF is a federation of sixty-two nonprofit organizations
whose aim is to promote better housing through cooperatives. It
was born in 1951 under the guidance of the Amalgamated Clothing
Workers of America, but its roots go back to the growth of the
first low-cost, union-sponsored housing cooperatives in the Bronx,
which were launched in 1926 by Sidney Hillman, Jacob S.
Potofsky, and Abraham E. Kazan, with initial financial support
from the Jewish Daily Forward Association. The second Amalgamated Coop, occupied in 1930, was as successful as the first,
influencing other groups to start coops of their own.

The passage of the 1949 Housing Act, which, among other provisions, extended Federal aid for slum clearance, was the catalyst
which inspired the establishment of the United Housing Foundation, with initial grants from the Edward A. Filene Fund, and
Kazan as president and Shirley F. Boden as secretary. In 1955,
Kazan completed his first UHF coop, the 123-family Mutual
Housing Association near the original Amalgamated Coop in the

Bronx. This was followed in 1956 by the 1,672-unit East River Houses, sponsored by both the International Ladies' Garment Workers Union and the United Housing Foundation—the first Title I Housing project in the United States—with the ILGWU providing the $15 million in mortgage money.

Since its formation, the United Housing Foundation has provided housing for over 30,000 families in New York City at a cost of over half a billion dollars, with thousands of additional units on the drawing boards. Inspired by the example of the United Housing Foundation, unions around the country have attempted to sponsor cooperatives.

Although the early union cooperatives did not practice exclusion, they had few black members; even today, the older coops have far fewer blacks than the new ones. Some of the newer cooperatives—for example, Rochdale Village in Queens, New York, with 5,860 families, and Co-op City in the Bronx, with 15,382 apartments—are well integrated, with about 25 percent black families in Co-op City and a higher percentage in Rochdale Village. Over the years, the advertising material of the United Housing Foundation has increasingly emphasized that all are welcome, regardless of race, color or creed.

One reason for the great attractiveness of the United Housing Foundation's coops has been the low room cost. In 1971, for example, the monthly cost per room at Rochdale Village was only $24, rising to approximately $31.50 in 1974 and $41.50 in 1976 including utilities.[2] At Co-op City in 1969, a typical three-bedroom apartment with terrace on the twelfth floor had a carrying cost of $171.25 a month, which included utilities, after an equity investment of $2,925, with higher or lesser cost depending on location, height, and exposure. As a result of a 16-percent increase in 1970,

2. The minimum income requirements at Rochdale Village in 1976 are:

For a one-bedroom apartment	$8,400
For a two-bedroom apartment	$12,000
For a three-bedroom apartment	$14,000

carrying charges rose to $198.82, including utilities. These charges were further increased by 20 percent in 1973—that is, to $241.66 per month. In April 1975, a $10.65 increase per room was initiated, bringing the carrying charges for a three-bedroom apartment to $341.77. However, Co-op City's equity investment of $450 per room has not been changed since its inception.

Inflation and rising operating costs have now pitched Co-op City residents against its Board of Directors, which recently resigned in the face of a well-organized rent strike. While residents feel that the Board has been unresponsive to their needs, the Board points to a series of measures that were hoped to reduce the impact of inflation. There are charges and counter charges and some merit to each side of the issue. Perhaps the current difficulties could have been avoided if years ago the big Co-op City mortgage had been split up into separate mortgages for each building. Had this been done, at least half of Co-op City's units would have secured mortgages at 3 percent per annum. Political factors worked against this, favoring a single mortgage which, at the current rate of interest, is more than 5 percent. This, in turn, required steep increases in monthly carrying charges and eventually triggered off the rent strike.

Today some coops, like so much other urban housing, are faced with the problem of loss of white demand as the schools in the neighborhood become heavily black. If coops are to resist the pressures that generate uniracial communities, they must introduce some thoughtful planning in order to maintain their interracial character. Unfortunately, most coops, like other groups, are inclined to ignore renewed trends toward segregation until schools in their areas turn predominantly black, and by then remedial measures are difficult to apply.

Minority percentages in New York coops vary tremendously. Warbasse Houses in Brooklyn, completed in 1965 with 2,585 apartments and a $23-per-room average carrying charge at the inception, was less than 1 percent black in 1971, while Co-op City in the Bronx, with a $29-per-room carrying charge, was approximately 20 percent black in the same year.[3] The ILGWU coop in the Chelsea section of Manhattan, also known as Penn Station South, completed in 1963 with an average monthly charge of $24 per room, was estimated to be about 3 percent black in 1971.

Rochdale Village, located in Queens on the site of the former Jamaica racetrack and adjacent to a minority section, was about 30 percent black in 1971. Its crime rate took an upward turn in recent years, despite the fact that the community maintains its own sixty-one-man police force augmented by an auxiliary police group composed of residents, and occasional building patrols organized by the tenants. Statistics show, however, that Rochdale's crime rate is significantly lower than in the surrounding neighborhood, and in the city as a whole. Nevertheless, fear and dissatisfaction with the local schools took its toll, and considerable white flight followed. When Rochdale Village opened in 1964, 4,500 families —that is, 77 percent of a total of 5,860 families—were white. This figure dropped to 45 percent—possibly even 40 percent—in January 1974. With some exceptions, most of the move-outs have been white and most of the move-ins black. This trend, in my view, might have been checked—and certainly could have been decelerated—if the United Housing Foundation had operated a vigorous affirmative program for maintaining Rochdale as a well-integrated community. Its efforts to stem the tide came too late. Where well-planned programs are initiated early, the staff and board of cooperatives or other housing developments are sometimes in a position to prevent a project from backsliding into uniracial minority housing, but the task is even more difficult if the development happens to be in the path of black expansion.

Another major sponsor of cooperative housing in the United States is the Foundation for Cooperative Housing (FCH). Unlike the United Housing Foundation, which is basically New York

3. By 1974, the percentage of blacks in Co-op City had risen to approximately 25 percent.

oriented (though UHF has a Chicago branch that has opened a six-hundred-unit major coop at the north end of Hyde Park, under the direction of Joyce Miller of the Amalgamated Clothing Workers), the FCH is nationally, even internationally, oriented. FCH has been responsible for the development of coops in dozens of cities throughout the country. Its service arm, FCH Services, Incorporated, was headed in its first nineteen years by Roger Willcox, a brilliant community planner and one of the prime movers of Village Creek in Norwalk, where he lives. Willcox now heads a new organization, Techni-Coop, Incorporated, which was set up to do innovative work in cooperative housing. FCH Services is headed by Jeffrey G. Spragens, a Washington attorney with a substantial housing background. Under his direction, FCH is expanding its services to include eight basic programs: development of new projects, property management, marketing services, condominium and cooperative conversions, community and home-owners' association services, international housing, state financing agencies, and rural housing programs.

FCH's chief objective remains the sponsorship of new housing cooperatives, thus helping dozens of builders throughout the country to plan and develop housing communities for cooperative ownership. While the trustees of the parent foundation provided sponsorship, FCH Services, Incorporated, gave technical guidance and assistance to builders and handled the sales, the organization, and often the initial management of the cooperatives. From 1956 through 1974, FCH sponsored more than 300 cooperatives, with more than 60,000 new units in urban and suburban communities in thirty-two states, in addition to managing more than 13,000 housing units.

At first, following the lead of UHF, most FCH cooperatives were intentionally integrated. Over sixty integrated communities were developed in cities that ranged from Washington, Cincinnati, Chicago, Kansas City, and Des Moines to Albuquerque, Phoenix, and the San Francisco area. However, under pressure to handle more and more housing—for several years FCH was selling over

8,000 cooperative housing units per year—the FCH organization was decentralized, and its regional directors began to pursue different policies. In the Detroit metropolitan area, for example, where FCH sponsored more than seventy cooperatives with over 20,000 units, some cooperatives are integrated, some are all white, and others are all black. In the Kansas City area, where FCH Regional Director Ernest Salvas pursued a more socially motivated policy, there was at least token integration in all cooperative units. Parade Park, in Kansas City, a 510-unit inner-city cooperative near the downtown urban renewal area, has only token white occupancy, and several suburban cooperatives have only token black occupancy. Other FCH regional directors made no effort at all to develop integrated housing. In Atlanta, for instance, segregation was retained to such a degree that the Urban League and other organizations joined in an examination of FCH's policy in that city; the inquiry was eventually dropped.

FCH's special expertise includes its skill in working with conventional or FHA builders, helping them to develop FHA-sponsored coops which require very little cash for downpayments. Many of these projects come under low-income programs, such as HUD's Section 236. FCH is also highly proficient in converting conventional rental housing into cooperative housing, working with an able team of attorneys, headed by David Krooth, who is Chairman of the Legislative Committee of the National Housing Conference and very influential in developing American housing legislation.

In the international field, until recently under the effective guidance of Wallace Campbell, FCH has assisted with the development of coops in many countries, especially in South America.

Other cooperative leaders have had their own independent organizations. One, Shirley Boden, developed with Ruth Senior the nine-hundred-unit Morningside Heights Cooperative, near Columbia University in New York City. In order to ensure the multiracial character of the community, a system of secret quotas was used. Boden, a very sensitive, able developer, has a deep dedication to interracial causes. He has developed a series of coops in and around New York City, working through the Middle-Income Housing Corporation and the Fund for Urban Improvement, which he organized.

In 1967, Paul Golz, one of FCH's first regional directors, who headed the West Coast operations, established the independent Mutual Ownership Development Foundation (MODF), which enjoys a broad sponsorship among cooperative groups on the West Coast. In recent years, MODF has developed more than twenty cooperatives throughout California, most of them integrated. Golz followed a somewhat different technique from other developers'. Under his leadership, MODF has sponsored nonprofit rental projects with 100-percent mortgages. These projects were converted to cooperative ownership only after they were completed and sold. In many respects, this was a simpler method than the presold approach FCH and UHF used for most of their housing. MODF ran into trouble, however, when the sales market proved to be softer than anticipated.

Among the earliest independent cooperatives was Bryn Gweled Homesteads in Southampton, Bucks County, Pennsylvania. This is a unique cooperative of eighty two- and four-acre lots, leased from the coop for 99 years. Roads, tennis courts, and a swimming pool are maintained by the residents; the houses are mostly contemporary and vary greatly in price. Bryn Gweled was organized in 1939 as an integrated community, but the NAACP's Philadelphia staff was unaware of its existence until almost ten years later, when the first black family joined the coop and shortly thereafter built a house. About fifteen black families now live in the community and form almost 20 percent of its population.

Another community, organized by the Friends Neighborhood Guild and the American Friends Service Committee, is the Friends Housing Coop, in a largely black neighborhood at Fairmount Avenue and Eighth Street, in North Philadelphia. Originally about one-third black in 1954, this coop has been stable for years at 50 percent black and 50 percent white. Its stability can be attributed, in part, at least, to the deep concern of the residents and management for maintaining a truly interracial community, and to the attractive gardens and fine site planning developed under its architect, the late Oscar Stonorov. The Friends Housing Coop, within the heavily black problem-ridden center of Philadelphia, has remained a tiny integrated island, virtually unknown even to the younger generation of housing leaders in the city.

Special Problems of Coops

The cooperative technique—that is, the banding together of a number of families for achieving certain common objectives—has been used by real-estate and landlord interests to unload hundreds of multifamily properties. Practically all of these "real-estate sponsored" cooperatives have been all-white, or virtually all-white housing developments. There are hundreds of such "cooperatives" in New York City; they serve upper-income families, and some are reported to have successfully excluded Jews, blacks, and Spanish-speaking families.

Ridgewood Gardens Coop, in Maspeth, Queens, is a middle-income cooperative in New York City with very few black residents. Following the assassination of Dr. Martin Luther King, Jr., in 1968, the Ridgewood Gardens Board of Directors voted to make every third apartment available for black occupancy when move-outs occurred. This proposal was greeted with massive hysteria. A meeting of all cooperators was called, and within forty-eight hours, 290 of the 372 families had signed a petition for a special meeting to remove the Board. The New York Division of Housing refused to send a community relations representative, and, predictably, the Board was removed.

Such incidents confirm my opinion that a legal attack ought to be made on all waiting lists that were developed before widespread publicity was given to the illegality of all housing discrimination decreed by the 1968 U.S. Supreme Court decision in the case of *Jones v. Mayer*. No really effective national program has been mounted by HUD to acquaint minorities with the fact that all housing is open and available to everyone. Until HUD launches a vigorous campaign over TV and radio advising minorities of their rights to live where they wish and supplying them with white testers to accompany them when seeking homes, existing waiting lists that fail to reflect a broad awareness of open-housing laws should be fought in the courts.

The process of developing cooperatives presents a number of problems. Many groups have found that it takes years before their plans get off the ground. As a result, the general procedure in recent years has been for housing professionals to organize coops by recruiting the membership after the planning has been completed and the sales begun. This means that most cooperators do not really participate until after they move into the development. Participation is, of course, not easy to organize in coops with thousands of members, but the one-member-one-vote rule is vital to future success and stability. Coops *can* effectively run their own affairs if the membership takes responsibility for being active.

The Challenge of the New Towns

Columbia

Gurney Breckenfeld's *Columbia and the New Cities,* published in 1971, should be read by all who wish to understand the role of new towns. The author traces the history of Columbia, Maryland, America's first successful new town, and concludes that both Ebenezer Howard and James Rouse, Columbia's developer, "were driven by the same essential idea: build just one garden city with love in its veins and others will surely find a way to repeat the achievement."

Breckenfeld's thoughtful presentation of the planning process includes a description of the first meeting with a panel of behavioral science experts who were to develop social objectives for Columbia. "For Rouse the first 'shaft of light' flashed when, after two days of desultory talk, housing economist Chester Rapkin argued, 'We're all taking the wrong approach. We've got to create an environment which will nourish the force of love.' "[4]

At Columbia, this "force of love" has created, in the words of James Rouse, an "authentic" city, based on wide-ranging social concerns. The physical environment of this new town, the end product of a long planning process that reflects Rouse's commitment to improve the quality of life, is uniquely conducive to generating a broad range of friendships and community relationships, a sense of responsibility leading to an active involvement of residents in community affairs, and a "racial openness" which would not have developed in suburbs or conventional urban communities. A survey of one thousand Columbia households conducted in 1973 revealed that 55 percent of its members had more friends of different races since moving to Columbia. It is these human or social achievements, the result of a carefully applied urban sociology, rather than its architecture and layout, that have reserved for Columbia a special place among the new towns planned in this country.

Columbia's maximum population is expected to reach 110,000 in 1981, spread out over seven villages clustered around an urban center. Of the city's 18,000 acres, 3,200 acres are reserved for parks, lakes, woods, golf courses and playgrounds. By 1974, Columbia had approximately 33,000 residents, of whom about 17 percent were black. All religions worship under one roof in the Interfaith Center. Amenities which cater to the educational, recreational, and economic needs of the inhabitants have been provided in large measure.

In general, residents, planners, and investors agree that, at its present stage of development, the experiment of creating a new town at Columbia has been successful. Unfortunately, however, the original objective of establishing a balanced community—that is,

4. G. Breckenfeld, *Columbia and the New Cities* (New York: Washburn, 1971), p. 253.

a culturally, racially, *and* economically diversified population—seems to be on the verge of becoming meaningless. "The economic mix originally planned for Columbia is rapidly disappearing," according to a survey conducted in May 1973, by the Columbia Association. "Instead of having all ends of the economic spectrum like any other city," an official at Columbia remarked, "what we have is an extremely wealthy community that is just getting wealthier."[5] The following statistics from the same survey tell the story: the average annual income for a white family was roughly $19,000 in 1974, and for a black family, somewhat higher—$22,000. Only 7 percent of Columbia's households earned less than $8,000. The cheapest single-family house available to home-seekers was $35,000; townhouses averaged about $50,000. The suspension of federal money for housing subsidies, and rapidly rising land and construction costs, have seriously jeopardized Rouse's original intention of providing at least 10 percent of low- and moderate-income housing. At the current rate of development, only 3 percent of Columbia's housing needs—that is, no more than a thousand units—will be subsidized when completed. "In practical terms," the Survey concludes, ". . . a large portion of the Columbia Association staff whose spouses aren't employed, low-salaried teachers, government officials, bank clerks and blue-collar workers will not be able to live in Columbia." In order to meet the requirements of its original low-cost housing quota, the Rouse Corporation is holding land in the hope that the freeze on subsidies will eventually be lifted. However, officials of both the Corporation and the Columbia Association admit that "as the city's growth continues much of the land that would be suited for low or moderate housing is being sold off to builders."[6] This has induced members of the Columbia Association to investigate other ways of raising money should federal funds fail to materialize. One of

5. B. Richards, "Columbia: Too Much Wealth," *Washington Post,* May 6, 1974.
6. Richards, *op. cit.*

their recommendations proposes their teaming up with either the State of Maryland or Howard County for a joint venture of subsidized low-cost housing. As a first step, the Columbia Association has floated a bond for $15 million—a remarkable undertaking for a nongovernmental body without municipal taxing power. This measure has been reinforced by a solid "A rating" for future bonding purposes. In addition, the Interfaith Housing Corporation, a union of church groups that has sponsored a large portion of Columbia's low-income housing, is also studying joint financial ventures involving state, county, and Columbia Association money. Rouse himself does not consider the present shortage of low- and moderate-income housing an irreparable flaw in Columbia's general record of success. During an interview in May 1974, Rouse stated that "a full spectrum of rents and prices only comes about when there is a full spectrum of homes of age and amenities. You can't build old homes"—which are the traditional recourse for families of small means. This defensive, and, it is to be hoped, temporary, retreat from Columbia's original objectives should not be allowed to divert the planning process from its basic principles, which encompassed the founding of a well-balanced community—not another wealthy suburb, but a place where, in James Rouse's words, anyone could live, "from company janitor to company executive."

Despite the federal government's freeze on housing subsidies, which has curtailed Columbia's goal of 10 percent low-cost housing, the town still has a greater range of income levels and more black residents than can be found in neighboring counties. The percentage of blacks in Columbia varies from near 4 to 5 percent in some townhouse sections and 25 percent in some of the more expensive areas, to about 40 to 45 percent in the subsidized units already completed. From time to time, it appeared that some unintentional black "islands" might develop, first in some high-cost single-family houses, and later in low-cost housing. This danger was averted not only through sheer hard work and consultations (in which I participated), but chiefly through affirmative marketing, which, directed toward more whites, focused on specific areas of high black concentration.

Today, Columbia is a successful community. This claim rests partly on the evidence of land sales, which in 1971 alone totaled $27 million, and on the fact that the town has begun to repay its $80 million debt. According to Rouse, the ultimate profitability of Columbia "is now expected to be greater than estimated in the original economic model. This larger return . . . will not come without additional drawbacks. . . . Our peak debt is a great deal higher than first projected, and it will take several more years than planned for the final profits to be realized. You cannot define with sufficient precision far enough in advance what the economic conditions are going to be, and thus investors have to gamble that a 15 to 20-year commitment of their funds will turn out to be a sensible use of that money."[7]

Columbia's success to date rests on the vision of James Rouse, a Baltimore mortgage banker, and his wife Libby. Their human approach to community planning was applied in the careful process of assembling such outstanding planners as William E. Finley and Morton Hoppenfeld, economist Robert Gladstone, real-estate sales genius Malcolm Sherman, and dozens of other associates, not the least of which is the Connecticut General Life Insurance Company and its former chairman, Frazar Wilde.[8] Others who gave vital leadership were Scott Ditch, for years Columbia's director of marketing and later its director of public information; John Levering, now a full-time sculptor and painter in Columbia, who for four years headed the Columbia Association, which owns all the open

7. T. Graham and J. F. Moon, "Making a City: Just One Chance," *Columbia Flier,* May 2, 1974.

8. Columbia has recently undergone a refinancing. According to *House & Home* of February 1975, the Connecticut General Life Insurance Co. took over a 6.2 percent interest held by the Manufacturers Hanover Trust Company. This gives the Connecticut General 53.3 percent interest while the Rouse Company retains its 46.7 percent holding.

spaces and represents the people of Columbia; and Richard Anderson, Columbia's long-time manager.

That Columbia could succeed in Howard County, south of the Mason-Dixon Line, midway between Baltimore and Washington, in an area that voted heavily for Wallace during the presidential election of 1968, is a tribute to the entrepreneurial genius of Rouse and to his mortgage banking firm, Rouse and Company.

While the financing of new towns raises many difficult problems, Columbia will make it easier for others to follow suit, especially if the current moratorium on federally guaranteed loans on new towns should be lifted. Another problem, as Edward Eichler and Marshall Kaplan have pointed out, is that the profit return on capital invested in large-size community developments may be too low for the high risk involved[9]—a problem which today should receive the most urgent attention.

Reston

Reston in Virginia is situated eighteen miles west of the District of Columbia, near Washington's Dulles Airport. Financially, it is not nearly as successful a new town as Columbia. The developer, Robert E. Simon, Jr., did a superb job of site planning but lost control, possibly because of a lack of detailed economic planning, when finances got out of hand. This factor, together with the 1966 money squeeze that dried up funds for mortgage loans, caused Gulf Oil to take control to protect its $15 million investment in Reston.

The new town is expected to have 75,000 inhabitants by 1980, and to be a center of employment for 30,000 people in a safe, clean, and attractive environment. According to figures compiled in the fall of 1973, its population by then was approximately 23,500, of whom 3,000 worked in Reston.

9. *The Community Builders* (Berkeley: University of California Press, 1967).

Reston was conceived as a country-city, and the town's master plan calls for seven villages whose diversity of land use, services, and social activities seems more urban than urban-rural. About 15 percent of the land is set aside for single-family homes on one-third- to three-acre lots, while clusters of townhouses, garden apartments, and high-rise buildings take up the bulk of the residential land. Roughly 42 percent of the grounds has been preserved for public use, of which 23 percent has been assigned for lakes, parks, woods, swimming pools, golf courses, tennis courts, ballfields, and hiking trails.

Simon's dream was that Reston should be a way to live rather than a mere place to live in. The creation of a well-balanced community, not just a suburban subdivision, was his goal. However, faced with conventional zoning laws, he found it necessary to formulate a new code of ordinances which would enable the planners to avoid the "diffusion [of Reston] into separate, unrelated hunks without focus, identity, or community life," that characterize so many towns and cities. The old zoning laws, according to Simon, "have helped produce chaos on our highways, monotony in our subdivisions, ugliness in our shopping centers. They are to blame for the whole neon-lighted wasteland that exists because of the subdivision's separation from commercial and recreational facilities."[10] Mixed land use, on the other hand, gives the developer greater flexibility, reduces the distance between home and workplace, shops and recreational establishments, and allows him to mix high-rise and garden apartments, stores and community facilities, commercial areas and housing, and tight clusters of buildings with open spaces.

In order to realize these goals, the Reston planners persuaded the Board of Supervisors of Fairfax County to pass new zoning ordinances, which in 1962 launched Residential Planned Community (RPC) into law.

10. *A Brief History of Reston, Virginia* (Reston, Va.: Gulf Reston, Inc., 1973), p. 11.

GOOD NEIGHBORHOOD

"Residential Planned Community zoning," in Simon's words, "permits us . . . to spread commercial areas, recreation and community facilities throughout the town. Thus our high density area is not located in the center of the town as it would be in a conventional community. Rather, we are creating a high density sinew running through the property. Although we have provided for a large town center, Reston will also contain seven village centers (one is completed). Each village center . . . serves as the focal point of the neighborhood. This arrangement makes possible the intimacy and friendliness of a small-town 'Main Street' in a community large enough to offer the advantages of city living."[11]

Reston has been hailed as "one of the most striking communities in the country" and has been praised as "a major breakthrough in suburban building." Lake Anne Village, the first completed of the projected seven villages, certainly deserves this accolade to architecture and planning. Spread around a 30-acre artificial lake of the same name, the village combines urbanity with the beauties and attractions of country living. Clusters of townhouses and a fifteen-story sixty-unit apartment building line the shores of the lake, and a plaza with shops, restaurant, library, and community center adjoins the lake at the end where boats can dock. Winding pedestrian walkways connect residential areas with the center, and no house is farther away than a pleasant ten-minute walk.

So far Reston has not attracted nearly as much industry as Columbia, nor has it planned adequately for housing for low-income residents. It is likely that such provisions would have been made if Robert Simon had been able to buy the site without the pressures of heavy payments on mortgaged land, and if more capital had allowed him to keep control of Reston. When Robert H. Ryan, a Pittsburgh real-estate consultant, took over from Simon, it became apparent that Simon's ideals would come

11. R. E. Simon, Jr., "Modern Zoning for Reston," *American County Government*, May 1967.

under fire. Criticizing Reston's design, prices, and attempt to mix low- and high-income families, Ryan declared: "The American ethic for two hundred years has been for income levels to live with their own kind."

Reston's industrial growth has been relatively slow: From thirty-three companies with 2,100 employees in 1970 it rose to one hundred eighty firms and associations with a working force of 3,000 by 1973. This is also true of Reston's population figures: In 1970, there were approximately 9,000 residents who occupied 1,096 rental units, 795 townhouses, and 620 detached single-family homes; by 1973, 23,500 residents lived in 3,000 rental units, 2,600 townhouses and condominiums, and 1,500 single-family homes for sale. Part of this relatively slow progress can be attributed to the absence of easy financing for home purchasing until Gulf Oil put up another $35 million—in addition to its original $15-million investment. Part of the new investment was used to provide 90-percent mortgages for home-buyers.

Residents are generally agreed that Reston's physical facilities —the plazas, walkways, community pools—have given the town a unique openness, an environment which encourages and achieves a high degree of social mixing. Despite a concentration of white middle-class, white-collar people, there is very little evidence of snobbishness, pretension, or clannishness. In fact, people seem anxious to meet others from different backgrounds.

Reston has a much lower percentage of black residents than Columbia, probably because of its higher price range and less easy access to the Baltimore and Washington markets. In the absence of reliable statistics, the consensus seems to be that roughly 7 percent of Reston's 23,500 inhabitants are black. There are no ghettos, no pockets of racial concentration. Black residents live everywhere in Reston, in low-cost subsidized housing as well as in high-value housing. The actual question of high percentage figures may be of less importance than the very welcome fact that "the black population involves itself in all of the social, cultural, and civic activities in Reston," as one resident put it.

By 1974, sales prices ranged from $26,500 for a two-bedroom/two-bath condominium to luxury homes that might sell for $172,000 to $250,000. Depending on the number of bedrooms and other features, the median sales price for a house was approximately $50,000. Reston does have a program of subsidized housing, including 236, 221 (d) (3), and Section 23 leased housing. The subsidized housing units completed by 1974 were composed of:

198 FHA 221 (d) (3) apartments
490 FHA 236 apartments
138 FHA apartments (a 9-story highrise for senior citizens)
200 FHA 236 apartment condominiums
287 FHA 236 town houses

Rents in the subsidized sector ranged from $123 to $153 for a one-bedroom apartment to $181 to $226 for a four-bedroom unit.[12]

Reston has a commitment to maintain a balance of 15 percent of its total housing units for low- and moderate-income families. If the 1974 trend of 18 percent can be sustained, this demand is likely to be met during the remaining years of construction. Current plans provide for an additional 759 subsidized housing units, but whether this rate of development can be maintained depends, of course, on the availability of government subsidies.

Bisecting the urban area, on a tract of over a thousand acres, is Reston's Center for Business and Industry. It includes about 180 businesses, light industries, and professional firms and associations, in addition to the Reston Sheraton Inn and the International Conference Center Complex, which provides the most extensive meeting and seminar facilities in Northern Virginia. Professional associations such as the National Education Association and the American Newspaper Publishers Association have selected Reston

12. These and the following figures were supplied by Gulf Reston, Inc., in May 1974.

for their headquarters, and the proximity of Dulles International Airport and government departments in Washington are obvious assets in attracting them.

The Reston business community provides clerical, industrial, and professional jobs, as well as a number of part-time jobs for working mothers. Large numbers of residents still commute out of Reston for work, a factor which is expected to change as more businesses, organizations, professional associations, and manufacturing firms find it advantageous to move to Reston. Improved mass transportation and the opening of the western access ramp to the Dulles Expressway will also contribute to the growth of business and employment opportunities, as will the completion of the national headquarters of the United States Geological Survey, which will provide 2,800 additional jobs.

There can be no doubt that Reston's exciting original planning will continue to attract a steady flow of both minority and white home-buyers. As to the town's financial problems, Robert Simon rightly declared some time ago, "We've created enormous land values by the quality of the development. The pot of gold at the end of the run will be equities (in apartments, stores, and industrial buildings) that will be paying for themselves out of earnings."[13]

New Towns-in-Towns

Urban facilities and cultural advantages should make the new towns-in-towns as workable and attractive as those new towns which now exist outside metropolitan areas. Plans for such new towns-in-towns are now in varying stages of development. Their developers hope to create a high-density, quality environment, a setting for healthful, stimulating, and socially rewarding living within the areas of central cities. An outstanding example of a

---

13. G. Breckenfeld, *op. cit.*, p. 142.

blend of urban renewal, a multidisciplinary approach to the planning process, and the application of the new-town-in-town concept is the Cedar-Riverside section of Minneapolis, Minnesota.

Cedar-Riverside is situated on the west bank of the Mississippi River, twelve blocks from downtown Minneapolis. Several major educational institutions, including the West Bank campus of the University of Minnesota, as well as two hospitals, are dispersed over its roughly 340 acres.

During the latter half of the nineteenth century, immigrants who were employed in the local lumber and milling industries built their homes in Cedar-Riverside, on the banks of the river. The population reached its peak with 12,000 residents, but then declined, according to the 1970 Census, to about 4,000. By 1938, Cedar-Riverside was considered ready for renewal. Various proposals were put forward to halt its deterioration, among others an analysis of conditions and the site's future potential published by the City Planning Commission of Minneapolis. This culminated in 1968 with the adoption of an urban renewal plan. Concurrently, to prevent the proliferation of small buildings that would seriously interfere with the planning process, private developers and local institutions had made substantial land acquisitions in Cedar-Riverside.

"Planning," according to the developers, "will incorporate the needs of the area for heterogeneous high-density housing types and sizes that are socially and economically integrated. . . . Developments must be well planned, architecturally and aesthetically coordinated, and of human scale, so as to meet the needs and growth of the surrounding institutions."

Cedar-Riverside Associates, Incorporated, the major private developer, began its career with small purchases of individual homes by Martin and Gloria Segal and Keith Heller, in 1964. Gradually, the Heller-Segal group acquired all the land in the eastern part of Cedar Village, while a Minneapolis real-estate firm, B. W. and L. Harris, assembled land in the western half. These two groups set up Cedar Village Associates for the purpose

of joint planning activities in the area. After the Urban Renewal
Plan had been adopted in 1968, the need for additional funds to
hold and continue land acquisitions became evident. Moreover,
the property assembled by the Harris group had to be acquired to
provide a single, coherent base for development. To achieve this
goal, Henry T. McKnight, the developer of the new town of
Jonathan in Minnesota, was asked to join the Segal-Heller group
along with a number of smaller investors. Cedar-Riverside Associates, Incorporated, was officially launched with the McKnight-
Segal-Heller group holding roughly two-thirds of the ownership,
and other investors approximately one-third.

Following the approval of the Urban Renewal Plan in 1968,
Cedar-Riverside Associates began work on comprehensive plans
for the 340-acre site. A multidisciplinary team of planners had
been brought together as early as 1966, including, among other
experts, Heikki von Hertzen, the founder of Tapiola in Finland.
In 1971, the Office of New Communities of the Department of
Housing and Urban Development approved a federal loan guarantee for Cedar-Riverside Associates to "assist in creating the first
federally designated 'New Town-in-Town' in the United States."

One hundred acres of the 340-acre site of Cedar-Riverside have
been set aside for private development. Here construction has
been phased out over a fifteen-to-twenty-year period to maintain
the "social fabric of the existing community."

Pedestrian and vehicular traffic will be separated by a system
of walkways and plazas. Some of the walkways, in particular those
close to public plazas, will be climate controlled. Others will be
elevated above the streets, giving access to and connecting the
upper levels of buildings. The walkways and the skyway system
will link residential areas with the institutions located in Cedar-
Riverside as well as with the commercial center and community
facilities. Some of the plazas or public squares are intended to be
placed on top of ramps. Pedestrian circulation will be further improved by an efficient use of stairs and elevators, and by a bridge
to connect the East Bank campus of the University of Minnesota

with the West Bank campus and thence with downtown Minneapolis. This kind of pedestrian circulation system, essential in a high-density urban community, will contribute effectively to preventing traffic congestion and easing the parking problem.

Cedar-Riverside's ten-stage plan provides for 12,500 dwelling units of different sizes and architectural styles, and for 1.5 million square feet of gross commercial space, as well as about six acres for cultural amenities that include several theaters. By 1990, Cedar-Riverside's population is expected to reach 30,000, with 5,000 persons living in housing related to its educational/medical institutions. A daily community-wide activity rate of approximately 60,000 people has been projected.

The first phase of the overall plan focused on the western part of Cedar Village, where some of the poorest, most run-down housing was located. Stage One of the plan, now almost completed, provides for 1,299 residential units with complementary service, commercial, and neighborhood facilities. About 75 percent of this section of Cedar-Riverside is occupied and reflects many of the elements contained in the overall plan. Cedar Square West, the completed first stage of the plan, offers residents a wide variety of housing that caters to the needs of a socially heterogeneous population. "There are 117 units of public leased housing, 552 units of federally subsidized 236 housing, 408 units of middle income housing and 222 units of semi-luxury housing. The FHA subsidized and unsubsidized housing will be integrated within the same building. To further achieve the objective of maximum choice for the individual, there are four basic unit types, five unit sizes and a rent range between $40 and $500 per month."[14]

According to a spokesman of Cedar-Riverside Associates, Incorporated, the rent schedule for 1976 is as follows: the lowest rent in the project is $20 for units designated as public housing,

14. Cedar-Riverside Associates, Inc., *Cedar-Riverside New Community*. Narrative Description. Revised September 26, 1973, P. 13. Also for the other quotations in this section.

which is supported by Section 8 of the Minneapolis Housing Authority. The highest rent in the same project is $466 per month for a four-bedroom apartment in the Section 220 semi-luxury units. All Section 8 leased public housing rentals are less than $120 per month.

Exterior architectural design does not in any way distinguish between low-, middle-, and high-income buildings. This allows people of all economic levels to live side by side in Cedar Square West, in identical apartments, on the same floors of the same buildings, although some rents are subsidized under Section 8 (formerly Section 236) while others conform to the current market rate. Minorities occupy about 15 percent of the buildings, which is almost three times the minority population average of Minneapolis. Cedar-Riverside provides an excellent example of how to affirmatively achieve economic and social integration. Almost half of Cedar Square West's residents are students or people otherwise connected with the community's medical/educational institutions. The other half comprises all types of professions and age groups. According to a spokesman of Cedar-Riverside Associates, "the economic integration experiment is working, but does require management control."

By 1990, the ten-stage development of Cedar-Riverside will be completed. Then this new town-in-town will stand as a self-contained city, with a prime commercial complex in an elongated center, convenience shopping distributed over a wide area, and cultural and educational amenities to assure a well-balanced and stimulating urban environment.

Although Cedar-Riverside received national acclaim and won a design award from the American Institute of Architects in 1975, criticism has also been voiced. Complaints are chiefly leveled against Cedar-Riverside's high density and high-rise construction which many residents find unsatisfactory as an environment for raising children. Three years after the completion of the first 1,299-unit section, Cedar-Riverside, like many other large-scale developments, faces serious financial problems. A lawsuit filed by a coalition of community groups in the United States District Court resulted in HUD being enjoined from advancing funds for Stage II of the project. The suit charged that HUD, the Minneapolis Housing and Redevelopment Authority, and Cedar-Riverside Associates had failed to adequately consider alternatives to the project's high-rise, high-density design, and that the government had submitted an inadequate environmental impact statement. HUD has appealed this decision.

Cedar-Riverside's positive features, such as low rents, the replacement of low-income segregation with a tenant population of mixed economic and social background, and architectural excellence are currently overshadowed by consumer objections. High-rise housing, especially for low- and moderate-income families, is generally under attack. But given the limited areas of new-towns-in-town and the number of people to be housed, what are the alternatives? Economic considerations—land values and the nature of financing construction—have determined, as in so many other developments, Cedar-Riverside's final form. The high cost of land made high-density building almost inevitable if the development was to be economically viable. True, the net cost of land could have been reduced if the developers had made more use of subsidies. They failed to do this to protect the investors who had joined Cedar-Riverside Associates for tax shelter. However, none of Cedar-Riverside's difficulties negate the new-towns-in-town concept. They merely demand a reappraisal of the exclusive use of high-rise, high-density housing for low- and moderate-income families with children.

The new towns, like other enterprises, are not immune to the effects of a contracting economy. Inflation and a depressed housing market have given the newly planned communities some tough sledding, aggravated by the fact that federal grants approved by Congress under the Urban Growth and New Community Development Act of 1970 have never been fully implemented. Without further government aid, some of the new towns built with HUD-approved loans might go bankrupt. Many urbanists and developers feel that HUD's "half-hearted approach in the past, . . . contributed to the present problems. The law, they point out, gives HUD much more authority to help new towns than simply guaranteeing loans, for which HUD collects sizeable fees from the developers. HUD can make direct low-interest, deferred-payment loans, for example, and it can make grants for planning and such necessities as sewers. But, except for a few grants early on in the program, HUD has failed to make use of this authority."[15]

Even Columbia, financially more successful than other new towns, feels the recession and finds it difficult to meet its payments to its main backer, the Connecticut General Life Insurance Company. The "precipitous collapse of the real estate industry," as James Rouse put it, accounts for the drop of land sales at Columbia, which averaged $24 million in 1971, 1972, and 1973, but only $6.5 million for the first five months in 1974. Connecticut General has now refinanced a $129-million loan to Columbia and has postponed the payment of principal and interest until July 1978.

The survival of the new towns thus depends more and more on full and unequivocal backing by the federal government. At present, it is the government which "is failing the new communities, not the other way round," according to the Howard Research & Development Corporation, the builders of Columbia. A shaky economy is not likely to favor the building of new towns on the scale of Reston and Columbia, although the development of new communities would revitalize the housing industry. Instead, smaller projects for fewer than 30,000 residents are more likely to be built by private developers who are heavily dependent on local governments and may not be able to command the capital larger developments require. To deal with this situation, Rouse has proposed the "creation of local and public community development corporations that could acquire, plan and market parcels of

15. *Business Week*, February 10, 1975, p. 43.

land and guarantee the extension of vital sewerage, water and roads, services that developers must be able to count on, but that are often completely out of their control."[16] In addition, home-seekers and housing consumers should make their voices heard through housing and planning associations, labor unions, churches, and fraternal orders, stating clearly that they want more than slumburbia to live in, and that the new towns should be for *all* people. The invisible economic integration which forms part of the success of Cedar-Riverside is the crucial ingredient for the planned communities of the future.

Housing for Reality

The time has long passed when we need to justify open housing in moral terms. We have seen how its alternatives create segregated schools, transform our cities into dying enclaves of poor minorities, and create suburbs that are beginning to repeat the old process all over again. In the long run, there is simply no one who profits from segregation; we are all losers. After decades of openly advocating housing discrimination and segregation, the federal government is now under a clear mandate to promote affirmative action for open housing. But the mandate requires reciprocal action by hous-ing consumers, private investors, builders and developers, as well as by the real-estate industry, if open housing is to take on more than token reality.

Some of the country's largest housing developers have found that the new generation of housing consumers has reversed the prejudices of its grandparents. Those developers who continue to exclude minorities now often find themselves involved in costly legal and public-relations struggles, which sap strength and capital from developments that once found it profitable to practice racial discrimination. Most of the young builders now heading housing

16. Graham and Moon, *op. cit.*

development firms across the country are committed to policies of open housing, not simply because the law requires it, but because they have come to recognize its profitability. They face the challenge of creating vigorous affirmative marketing programs, and implementing these programs in the lower echelons of their firms, where the old exclusionary practices flourish.

Concurrently, the great majority of black citizens have not been diverted by those working to profit from the status quo and to preserve it: they are aware that most programs for "black capitalism" merely seek to polish the ghetto, and that there is simply no substitute for decent housing in open communities.

The housing realities of the 1970s, for developers, brokers, government, and consumers alike, have been dramatically presented by the findings of a social audit conducted by the Massachusetts Housing Finance Agency (MHFA).[17] Since 1966, MHFA has actively promoted the financing of low, moderate, and middle-income housing, and has closed and committed loans for over 30,000 housing units throughout the commonwealth of Massachusetts. With a mandate to promote economic integration that required it to be accountable for its policies to a wider public, the agency took steps to test the results of mixed-income occupancy in MHFA developments. It decided to sponsor "a factual analysis by an outside source to measure the effectiveness of its program." Does a development with a homogeneous income level and a uniracial population produce more satisfied residents than one with a heterogeneous structure? An independent research team was hired to find out.

In the early stages of their inquiries, the researchers found that income or racial mix were neither the sole nor the determining factors of "tenant satisfaction." They thus devised a more comprehensive conceptual model, which included such variables as quality

17. *All In Together: An Evaluation of Mixed-Income Multi-Family Housing* (Boston: Massachusetts Housing Finance Agency, 1974). Also for the following quotations.

of design and construction, location of the development, demographic characteristics, mix and scope of subsidies, "judgments of reactions to the new development, rental policy with respect to screening and receptivity to minorities," and management practices and style. Once they recognized that the effect of economic and racial integration could be adequately assessed only within the context of a wider framework, it was hoped that these variables might be "meaningfully correlated with tenant satisfaction, as well as with each other."

The team focused their study on sixteen MHFA developments, with a total of 3,200 households. The developments consisted chiefly of garden-type apartments located both in suburbs and in small towns and cities in Massachusetts. Rehabs and recently financed high-rise housing in the larger central cities were excluded from the survey. The researchers conducted intensive interviews with a representative group of 197 residents of the sixteen MHFA developments, and with 125 tenants of a comparison group. They determined that this sampling procedure reflected fairly accurately the general views of other Massachusetts residents in "similar multi-family housing at three income levels: conventional-market developments; 236 developments; and public housing." In addition, the team undertook a detailed analysis of the 3,200 households and the history of each development, as well as a quantitative analysis of the neighborhood in which the development was located.

The findings showed that a "broad income mix works in these MHFA developments, *producing higher levels of satisfaction at all levels*—market, moderate-income, and low-income—*principally because these developments are superior in design, construction and management*" (the italics are mine). More specifically, 89 percent of the residents in the MHFA developments were "very satisfied" or "just satisfied" with their living conditions, as opposed to only 78 percent of the comparison group. "Tenant satisfaction," it was found, is "only indirectly and in a secondary fashion" related to matters of residents' income and racial mix. The Report concluded that "income mix, surely, and racial mix, very probably, have no significant effect on satisfaction; whatever conceivable effect they might have is overwhelmed and completely over-shadowed by more basic factors of design, construction, space, facilities, location, maintenance and management." The most common response to whether a development should be more hetero-geneous in regard to race, income and age groups, was indifference; residents who did specify a preference for a greater variety were more numerous than those who preferred "similarity."

Once perceived, these findings are almost blindingly logical. Their simple common sense should be enough to convince us that the prejudices of the past have become the self-fulfilling prophecies of the future. Neighborhoods and schools which are *expected* to decay will undoubtedly do so—unless we act as if we expect them to survive and flourish, and provide the kind of nourishment they need to do so. The way for affirmative action is clear, and so is the necessity. Let us break the cycle now.

Appendix

Recommendations to Promote Racial Integration in Housing

Morris Milgram, President, Planned Communities, Inc. and Roger N. Beilenson, Assistant to the President, Planned Communities, Inc.

This study was conducted pursuant to contract H-926 with the Department of Housing and Urban Development on behalf of the National Commission on Urban Problems, appointed by the President and chaired by the late Senator Paul H. Douglas

Summary

. . . the concerned white man who desperately reaches out across the barriers of color rediscovers his own humanity.—*Psychology Today,* June 1968.

In order to promote open occupancy in housing and widespread racial integration, we believe that:

1. Individuals must act for integration, not for segregation, when they select housing. As the new fair housing pledge of the National Committee on Tithing in Investment (NCTI) states: white persons should

try to find housing on a block where Negroes already live (while Negroes should) try to find housing on a block where Negroes do not live, far from areas of Negro concentration.

Moves by whites into areas from which Negroes are barred by de facto exclusion, accomplished by numerous stratagems including lies and threats, strengthen American Apartheid and hasten the day when our cities will be completely segregated.

Individuals in leadership positions have a great responsibility to move so as to reduce ghettoization, because they are looked to as examples by the rest of the population.

2. Civil liberties, civil rights, fair housing and similar groups must recognize that it is not sufficient to work for progressive legislation, support law suits, and aid Negroes in finding unsegregated housing. They must educate their memberships to live their beliefs by making moves which foster integration.

3. Businesses, voluntary organizations, churches, universities and foundations—and government agencies as well—must give financial support to fair housing centers, neighborhood stabilization groups and educational efforts such as that of NCTI.

4. Investments in housing open for all, both under private financing and under Federal and State low and moderate income housing programs, must be made by individuals of means and by voluntary, educational and religious organizations and union pension funds, both as risk capital and as mortgage financing. Private business corporations and individuals can make such investments using free capital and treasury stock. If made imaginatively, they can thereby derive considerable tax shelter leaving them more tax-free spendable cash while achieving vital social goals.

5. The housing supply in predominantly white areas, in particular housing for persons of low and moderate incomes, should be greatly increased, by offering adequate economic incentives to real estate builders and developers to construct such housing open to all.

6. Owners of existing and new multi-family housing in substantially all-white areas who integrate their buildings should receive mortgage financing incentives, such as 90% of value, long term low interest loans, insured by the Federal Housing Administration (FHA).

7. Developers of subdivisions of one to four-family houses in substantially all-white areas who integrate their developments

should receive similar construction financing incentives from FHA.

8. A publicly-owned National Open Neighborhoods Housing Corporation should be formed to purchase housing in predominantly white areas and open up such housing to members of minority groups, and to purchase housing and stabilize tenancies in integrated neighborhoods.

9. The U.S. Department of Housing and Urban Development should vigorously and effectively implement existing non-discrimination and open occupancy regulations; in particular, FHA should require affirmative integration programs by developers having FHA-insured loans and should affirmatively provide for integration of repossessed housing.

10. Federal action to stabilize integrated neighborhoods should be taken. Government at all levels should greatly increase expenditures for schools and other community facilities in these areas. Government should support private stabilization and improvement efforts.

11. Federal law and administrative practice should be changed to provide economic incentives under Federal programs such as public housing, urban renewal and model cities to stimulate localities to racially integrate their housing.

12. Major government contractors should be required to ensure that suitable housing reasonably near their plants is available for minority group employees as well as for whites.

13. Moves that aid Federal housing policy—decreasing ghettoization and urban sprawl—should be encouraged by giving 98% FHA loans to families who make such moves.

14. All tax exempt institutions should be required, as a condition of continuing exemption, to invest at least 5% of their investment capital in properties financed under Federal and State programs for low and moderate income families.

15. A computerized clearinghouse of houses and apartments available for sale or rental should be set up by FHA to guide returning veterans and others to housing accommodations where their moving would strengthen Federal housing policy.

APPENDIX

Recommendations to Promote Racial Integration in Housing

Introduction

Large-scale racial integration in housing requires (1) total open occupancy allowing minorities complete access to all housing in America; (2) voluntary stabilization of integrated areas on the periphery of minority areas; and (3) integration of areas of minority concentration through construction of large new areas for total living and working.

Total open occupancy would provide the way to achieve a true American multi-racial society. It would give minorities the ability to live anywhere in the nation and to follow the jobs that are increasingly moving to the outskirts of the central city and to the suburbs.[1] The presence of minority residents in more than token numbers in presently all-white areas would remove some of the social pressure on white inner-city residents to leave integrated areas. Finally, open occupancy would give minority families a much greater opportunity to own their own homes.

Stabilization of already racially mixed neighborhoods on the periphery of the ghetto requires that there be open occupancy in white areas for all minorities, and that whites be willing to stay in and move into integrated areas. Stabilization is particularly important because it is in integrated areas that blacks experience their first contact with white neighbors. White flight from these middle-class neighborhoods creates in the Negro middle class residents a feeling of profound hopelessness of ever achieving acceptance in America as equals under the present system; subsequently, hatred of the white man is bred as a result of the refusal to recognize the black man's individual worth.

The Kerner Report points out the danger of complete polarization of the races, and we are rushing toward the collision of the two segments of our society. Therefore, to avoid continuation and intensification of the American Apartheid which threatens to destroy our social fabric, it will be necessary to develop imaginative programs, backed by substantial Federal and private financial resources, which will encourage integration. It is totally unrealistic to believe that laws against housing discrimination can alone overcome centuries of prejudice, ignorance and fear.

These integration programs would include the giving of adequate financial incentives to the real estate industry to sell and rent housing in presently all-white areas to minority group persons and the establishment of a National Open Neighborhoods Housing Corporation which would purchase and integrate the tenancy of housing in all-white areas, and in integrated areas as well. In all areas, new housing for persons of varying incomes must be constructed; this could be accomplished in some cases through urban renewal. With respect to already integrated areas, substantial Federal moneys must be made available to upgrade school quality and, through use of educational parks and special enrichment programs, to combat racial imbalance in the schools. Also, metropolitan transportation systems must be markedly improved, and community safety improved through cooperative programs bringing together the police and community residents.

Special Federal incentives and financial commitments to increase and sustain residential racial *integration* are fully justified. For many years, the Federal Government actively worked to increase and sustain residential racial *segregation* as a positive good. As housing expert Charles Abrams states in *Forbidden Neighbors,*

. . . FHA adopted a racial policy that could well have been culled from the Nuremberg laws.[2]

In 1938, the official Federal Housing Administration *Underwriting Manual* cautioned home-buyers that:

If a neighborhood is to retain stability, it is necessary that properties shall continue to be occupied by the same social and racial groups.[3]

And, although official Government policy now supports racial integration and non-discrimination, actual practices by the Department of Housing and Urban Development (HUD) in large measure have the opposite result, as outlined by the National Committee Against Discrimination in Housing in *How the Federal Government Builds Ghettos*.[4]

The following programs are recommended:

A. Expansion of the Housing Supply

Expansion of the housing supply in predominantly white areas, particularly housing which can be afforded by households with low or moderate annual incomes, is absolutely essential to achieve significant racial integration and deghettoization.[5]

Although the details of how to achieve such an expansion are beyond this study's purview, we are convinced that the key to facilitating the integration of the housing supply is the offering by the Federal Government of *adequate economic incentives* to *profit-making builders and developers* who agree to construct the kind of housing the Government wants, where it wants it, and at a cost and rental level approved by the Government, the effect on racial integration being an important criterion. Provision of housing for low and moderate income families is a national necessity; private enterprise deserves a realistic profit if it serves this need.

Present Federal low income and moderate income programs, such as low rent public housing, leased public housing, rent supplements and the moderate income housing programs, should be funded at a high level and should be strengthened.

Practices engaged in by local municipalities (especially in the suburbs) which prevent developers from constructing housing for all income levels should be restricted. All too often in the past, the zoning, eminent domain and taxing powers have been used to preserve localities as wealthy, all-white retreats.

Some of such new housing should be in racially and economically inclusive New Towns. As General Eisenhower recently stated:

. . . The first essential of any realistic housing plan is to reduce the density of population by encouraging large numbers of people to relocate in new, more wholesome communities. . . . They must be open, and made inviting, to decent people of all races.

. . . I know of no better way to restore vanished hope and pride in the hearts of hundreds of thousands of despairing people.[6]

Substantially increasing the housing supply will make much more fruitful other strategies designed to accelerate racial integration in existing housing, especially the mortgage financing incentive programs described in subsection B below.

B. Mortgage Financing Incentives

1. To Owners of Existing Multi-Family Housing

Massive numbers of newly-constructed, Federally-aided or State-aided housing units located in predominantly white areas cannot be completed in less than 3–5 years. Especially prior to that time, efforts should be made to make presently existing housing available to minority households.

Again, in our judgment, massive amounts of existing multi-family housing would be made available to minority groups only if, in return, owners of such housing were offered adequate economic incentives to show that integrated housing would be clearly more profitable than uniracial housing.

We therefore recommend that the owner of any apartment house having 10 or more units and located in a neighborhood which has a percentage of non-whites less than the percentage of non-whites in the national population at the last Census (such neighborhoods to be defined by HUD) be given specified financing aids if the building's tenancy includes a percentage of non-whites greater than the percentage of non-whites in the national population but less than a majority.

These financing aids could be the following: First, FHA could guarantee a maximum 40 year mortgage loan equal to 90% of

FHA-appraised value of the land and building, at a market rate of interest. An insurance premium, as in all FHA loan guarantees, would be charged to defray administrative costs and to fund a reserve for any losses due to foreclosure. This would require refinancing by the owners.

Second, FHA could, without any refinancing being effected, directly subsidize the owner by reimbursing him for a portion of the interest payments made each year with respect to his mortgage loan. Thus, just as the owner of rental housing who operates his project for low and moderate income families would receive an interest subsidy under Title II of the proposed Housing and Urban Development Act of 1968,[7] the owner of an existing apartment who integrates racially would receive such an interest subsidy. Unlike the mortgage guarantee, such an incentive is a direct cost to the Government. A 1% interest subsidy relating to buildings having a total of 500,000 minority households would cost about $250–350 million annually.

These incentives could be used separately or in combination.

Congress would set the 90% of appraised value limitation and would determine the maximum interest subsidy, perhaps the difference between interest payments at the market rate of interest and interest payments on a 1% loan. FHA would by regulation specify the maximum mortgage term it would insure for the particular property involved, depending on the age and condition of the property. FHA would determine criteria under which property owners would be eligible for full or partial subsidies, and should be guided in setting such criteria by the need to offer substantial monetary incentives in order to achieve rapid, widespread integration.

Eligible geographical areas would be determined by HUD, using Census tract and block information from the last decennial or special Census. Special censuses could be taken in areas undergoing racial change. Incentives would be made available only with respect to buildings with at least 10 housing units. This requirement could be relaxed for urban areas which do not have a significant number of large apartment houses.

In the initial period, incentives should be limited to buildings which have a non-white tenancy at least equal to the national percentage of non-whites but less than a majority and which are in areas having a non-white percentage less than the national percentage. Periodically, both the area and tenant eligibility should be reevaluated in light of the program's purpose. A variant of the program for stabilization areas is needed.

In applying for mortgage financing incentives, the owner would submit evidence to HUD that his building qualified under the area and integration standards. He would also submit evidence that he is not attempting to evade the FHA requirements for new construction, such as physical inspections, equal opportunity in employment and payment of prevailing wages.

The owner must agree to implement an affirmative action program, including employment of minority group personnel and, where feasible, advertising in local minority press, to prevent the non-white percentage of tenants from falling below the national average. HUD should prescribe appropriate rollbacks of the mortgage aids if the owner, or subsequent owner, has not continued to make effective integration efforts and the non-white percentage falls for a year below half the required minimum.

The mortgage incentive program will have much greater social usefulness if it is designed so as to afford low income minority group families opportunity to participate (given the generally moderate to high rentals in many predominantly white areas).

As experience in the 221(d)(3) program indicates, the granting of mortgage financing incentives, sometimes even coupled with real estate tax abatement, is not sufficient at a 3% interest rate to permit the private owner of a development to rent apartments at levels low income people can afford (roughly, up to $80 monthly).

We believe that a rent supplement technique is required, similar to that utilized in the section 23 leased public housing program. Under that program, the local housing authority leases apartments in a private building owned by a non-profit or limited profit company and pays the owner the normal economic rent, at the same time receiving from the low income tenant (who has applied for public housing) an amount equal to 25% of his annual family income. The difference is subsidized by the Federal Government.

In this instance, the rent supplement should be granted by HUD directly to the private tenant, without recourse to the local housing authority at all. A low income person would apply for housing directly from a private landlord (profit-making, limited profit or non-profit), without applying for public housing. The low income person would then certify his income to the landlord, who would forward the certification (together with a signed lease) to HUD for approval of the necessary rent subsidy.

As an alternative to mortgage financing assistance, owners of buildings which qualify by area and integration of tenancy might be afforded a credit against local real estate taxes equal to perhaps $15 per month per apartment in the building so long as the necessary integration was maintained. The Federal Government would reimburse the municipality for the real estate tax loss.

2. To Developers of New Multi-Family Housing

The developer of any new apartment house having 10 or more units and located in a neighborhood having a percentage of non-whites less than the percentage of non-whites in the national population at the last Census should receive automatic interest subsidization during time periods in which the building's tenancy includes a percentage of non-whites greater than the percentage of non-whites in the national population but less than a majority.

With respect to FHA-insured properties, such an automatic interest rate subsidy can be written into the basic agreement to take effect when integration is achieved. In other cases, FHA should by regulation specify what types of properties, as to rental levels and so forth, would be eligible.

3. To Developers of New Sales Housing

The developer of any subdivision of one to four-family houses, having a first section of at least 10 dwelling units and located in a neighborhood having a percentage of non-whites less than the percentage of non-whites in the national population at the last Census, should be given construction financing aids if a percentage of such dwelling units greater than the percentage of non-whites in the population but less than a majority is sold to or occupied by non-whites.

FHA could give a rebate equal to 1–2% of the interest paid with respect to the construction loan. It could also, with respect to the next section of the development, guarantee a construction loan for a higher than usual percentage of cost, and could subsidize the interest rate on the loan. As each section is completed and occupancy is racially integrated within the approved limits, financing aids on the next section, or the developer's next subdivision, would be granted.

Owners of houses in qualifying single-family subdivisions might be granted interest subsidies on their mortgages and extension of the term of their mortgage loans.

4. To Purchasers of Existing Houses

The purchaser of any existing single-family or two-family house, whose purchase is in accordance with Federal housing goals as outlined by Congress, should be eligible for an FHA-insured loan up to a maximum of 98% of purchase price, including closing costs.

Federal housing policy should encourage residential racial integration where individual blocks would have a percentage of non-white residents at least equal to the percentage of non-whites in the national population but not more than three times that percentage. Federal housing policy should also encourage commutation to work of a maximum of 20 miles.

Persons who buy houses less than 20 miles from their work in such a way as to contribute to the achievement or maintenance of racial integration on their block would be eligible for the special FHA financing. Once 10% of the houses on a block had secured such financing, all other homeowners on the block who are less than 20 miles from work and whose presence aids racial integration would be eligible for such financing as well.

Decreasing ghettoization would decrease the feeling of hopelessness in the ghettoes and thus decrease costly racial unrest. Reducing long commutes to work would lessen the need for heavy Federal expenditures for roads, smog control, and sewer and water extensions.

C. National Open Neighborhoods Housing Corporation

We recommend that Congress charter a National Open Neighborhoods Housing Corporation.

This Corporation would be non-profit, have a Board of Directors appointed by the President, be empowered to purchase and own real property, and be funded by Congress and receive guarantees of financing by FHA. Its primary role would be to purchase existing housing in predominantly white areas and open up this housing to members of minority groups. A second major role would be to help stabilize already integrated areas on the periphery of the ghetto.

Racial integration on the scale required can be achieved as a by-product of new construction and through the mortgage financing incentives set forth above. Nevertheless, there is great need for an instrument designed specifically to implement a public policy of achieving racial integration in housing. This Corporation would act in precisely those areas and in those ways which would achieve maximum effect. For example, it could purchase apartment houses and single-family houses in all-white areas where there is little or no new construction under Federal programs or use of the mortgage financing incentives. The Corporation would be empowered to sell properties as it sees fit, to tenants' cooperatives and condominiums and to other entities.

Use of the Corporation as a "cutting edge" is stressed because it cannot as a practical matter purchase enough existing housing to begin to solve problems of residential segregation and ghettoization.[8] It is the quality of the Corporation's efforts that would count; its purchases should help to open up entire areas to minority families. Nevertheless, a massive effort to purchase and integrate housing should be mounted.

The Corporation should be non-profit. It is, unlike the National Housing Partnerships described in Title IX of the proposed Housing and Urban Development Act of 1968, not designed to encourage direct participation by private enterprise in solving segregation problems.

The Corporation is expressing the public interest. Its Board of Directors should be appointed by the President. Regional, ethnic and occupational factors should be given weight in choosing directors. The Board should have expertise in real estate and in social and inter-group problems.

The Corporation's administrative expenses should be funded by Congress, except as offset by cash flow from operations.

Financing would be provided by empowering FHA to guarantee loans to the Corporation equal to 100% of cost of the property, for a term of 50 years, at market rates of interest. If mortgage money is not available from private lenders, Fanny May [Federal National Mortgage Association] should be empowered to make loans to the Corporation.

The Corporation could provide housing for persons of moderate and low income in several ways. First, it could purchase existing housing which it would be economically feasible to operate under the section 221(d)(3) moderate income housing program, and apply for a reduction of the interest rate on its loan to 3% (or to 1% if the proposed interest subsidy program is enacted). The present HUD regulation limiting below market interest rate loans on existing property to those which are rehabilitated should be waived as to property owned by the Corporation.

Second, to provide for low income persons, it would be necessary to utilize a form of rent subsidy or supplement, as discussed in section B, above.

One special function that the Corporation might perform is the purchase and integration of new housing in New Towns. Developers of New Towns might construct such housing under a "turnkey" arrangement by which at completion of construction the housing, single family or multi-family, would be sold to the Corporation at an agreed price.

Since the Corporation would own housing in all-white areas, it would very likely have the problem of attracting Negroes and other minorities as tenants. The Congressional appropriation of administrative expenses should include funds to attract minority tenants through an "outreach" program conducted either by the Corporation or under contract by real estate brokers having a reputation for non-discrimination, metropolitan fair housing centers, intergroup relations agencies or anti-poverty centers.

The Corporation could be organized as a separate entity or *its functions could be performed by one department of a National Housing Development Corporation.* Such a corporation, patterned after New York's Urban Development Corporation, would have the power to acquire property by eminent domain and to construct new housing for moderate and low income households under existing Federal and State programs. It would act in cooperation with local governments and existing neighborhood and community corporations and organizations which show a commitment to act in this field.

D. Federal Action to Ensure Open Occupancy

Federal housing policies have in the past promoted the creation of the suburbs as a white noose strangling the central cities. Now, the Federal Government must take affirmative action to ensure that the suburbs and other all-white areas become integrated. We recommend:

1. *Vigorous, effective implementation of HUD's present regulations regarding non-discrimination and freedom of choice for minority groups, and any further regulations which are adopted,*

through an expanded and strengthened equal opportunity section. As experience under various strong State open housing laws clearly demonstrates, such laws and regulations by themselves have limited impact, and strong enforcement is *absolutely essential.* In this regard, a strengthened FHA Homeownership Counseling Service should educate minority group families as to filing of complaints of discrimination.

2. Issuance of an FHA Commissioner Letter requiring that each developer receiving the benefit of an FHA mortgage loan guarantee (including "New Town" developers) implement an affirmative program to attract non-white purchasers or tenants. Such a program could include employment of minority group salesmen or rental agents, and advertising in media reaching minority groups.

3. Adoption of an affirmative integration program by FHA with respect to repossessed single-family and multi-family dwellings. FHA should, where feasible, integrate such areas or dwellings prior to disposition. Disposition should be made not solely so as to minimize loss to FHA but also to maximize social benefit. Disposition of multi-family units at low prices to local housing authorities, non-profit organizations or profit-making companies with a record of integrated tenancies would make housing available for moderate and low income persons, on an integrated basis. With respect to single-family houses, special efforts should be made to dispose of houses in white areas to minority families.

E. Federal Action to Stabilize Integrated Areas

Preservation of the integration which is already in existence—mainly in areas on the periphery of the ghetto which may be in racial transition—is extremely important. To stabilize such areas, we recommend:

1. Total open occupancy programs to lessen the demand of minorities to live in such areas, due to other areas being closed to them.

2. Purchase, by the National Open Neighborhoods Corporation,

of strategically located multi-family apartments in such areas, and maintenance of stable integration in these buildings.

3. Granting of incentives to white persons who remain in or move into such areas (see F.5 below).

4. Expenditure by Federal, State and local governments of substantially greater amounts to improve schools in stabilization areas, to reduce school racial imbalance where necessary, to provide a high degree of personal safety, and to provide parks and recreation, community facilities and other amenities. Such areas can be stabilized only if they are attractive, high quality neighborhoods. In the administration of Federal grant programs, special consideration must be given to already integrated areas.

5. Private stabilization and improvement efforts should be funded by the Government.

F. Other Recommendations

1. Public Housing and Metropolitanization

We recommend:

a. Amendment of Federal and State laws and regulations (where necessary) to enable local public housing authorities to rent or purchase available private housing outside the local jurisdiction (central city, in many cases) for low income families. Suburban governments should not have a veto power over agreements between a central city housing authority and private landlords to provide private housing for low income people. The locality has a legitimate concern about the physical quality of structures within its borders but does not have the right to exclude persons because of their income.

b. Metropolitanization of housing authorities so that public housing can be constructed anywhere in a region to provide for persons of low income living in all parts of the region. All areas within the region would have appropriate representation on the Authority. State law could mandate metropolitanization[9] and

Federal law could give priority to projects of metropolitan housing authorities. The details of establishing a metropolitan housing authority would have to be carefully considered.

c. Expansion of leasing by local housing authorities from FHA of repossessed single-family and multi-family dwellings.

d. Authorization to HUD to make capital grants to local housing authorities to "write down" the cost of land and site development costs in excess of the reuse value of the improved land for public housing which is not in urban renewal areas. Presently, the write down is greater for urban renewal areas, which tend to be located in areas of minority concentration, and a local housing authority should be given greater incentives to build a project outside such areas.

e. Giving priority to public housing projects which are located outside areas of minority group concentration. Projects within these areas perpetuate the second class status of minorities.

2. Moderate Income Housing

We recommend:

a. Authorization, under Federal moderate income housing programs including the 221(d)(3) program, to make provision for low income families by use of appropriate amounts of rent supplement funds and "Section 23" leasing of apartments by the local housing authority, so that up to one-third of the tenants could be low income. Under present law, only 5% of the rent supplement appropriation may be expended in 221(d)(3) housing. At the present time, the sponsor of a 221(d)(3) project may lease apartments to the local housing authority only if he is unable to rent up completely to moderate income families; he is, however, not permitted to include leasing to the housing authority to show, before the fact, that the project is marketable.[10]

b. Authorization to permit cooperatives and non-profit and limited profit corporations which acquire good quality existing apartment houses to refinance such properties under section

221(d)(3) without requiring that rehabilitation be performed. The present HUD regulation limits the amount of the permissible below market interest rate mortgage to five times the cost of new improvements (that is, to qualify for a 100% mortgage, rehabilitation equal to 20% of the cost including improvements would have to be done). The owner would, of course, upon receiving the new mortgage, have to comply with the 221(d)(3) requirements as to rent scales, income levels of tenants and so forth.

c. Authorization of the Secretary of HUD to waive the workable program requirement as a precondition to construction in a community of rent supplement housing and housing under 221(d)(3) if he is satisfied that such projects would be appropriate as planned. At the present time, suburban communities can forestall the construction of such needed housing simply by not submitting an acceptable workable program to HUD.

3. Urban Renewal and Model Cities

We recommend that incentives be given to those communities that implement (not plan) a program of substantial desegregation of minority group persons as part of urban renewal or Model Cities programs. Such incentive might take the form of an extra payment equal to 5% or 10% of the Federal grant made with respect to the particular project.

4. Government Contracts

We recommend that companies receiving major government contracts be required not only to have an affirmative program of hiring minority group persons but to ensure that suitable housing reasonably near the plant is available for minority group employees. This would be accomplished by ensuring open occupancy in local communities and, where necessary, by taking steps to see that new housing for low and moderate income people is constructed.

APPENDIX

5. Investments of Tax-Exempt Institutions

We recommend that institutions exempt from Federal income tax under section 501 of the Internal Revenue Code be required, as a condition of continuing exemption, to invest a specified percentage of their investment capital (5% the first year of program, 7½% the second year and 10% thereafter) either as equity or as mortgage loans, in properties financed under Federal or State programs for low and moderate income families in integrated areas. Institutions with less than $1 million of invested funds would be exempt.

6. Bank Investments

We recommend that banks affiliated with the Federal Reserve System be required to maintain a specified percentage of their assets (perhaps 2%) in government-insured mortgages on properties constructed for low and moderate income families.

7. Computeahome

We recommend that FHA set up a computerized clearinghouse of houses and apartments available for sale or rental in several metropolitan areas. Landlords, real estate brokers and owners could list with such a service only if they adopt non-discrimination policies in all transactions and if all listings are listed with the service. Members of the armed forces and Federal employees might be able to use the service free of charge and other persons would be charged a modest fee. The central computer would be tied into sending and receiving devices located in large department stores, anti-poverty centers, on military installations and at other convenient locations.

While matching the consumers' needs with respect to location, price or rental and so forth, the computerized recommendations would also reflect the social goal of achieving racial integration and could describe the community amenities of integrated areas.

If the clearinghouse proves to be successful, it should be provided in every major metropolitan area.

8. Support of Private Integration Efforts; Attraction of Negro Families to White Areas

We recommend:

a. Government financial support for regional fair housing centers in every major metropolitan area. These centers, having integrated staffs and with branch offices in areas of minority group concentration, should be relied upon for the "outreach" effort necessary to identify minority persons able and willing to move to predominantly white areas.

Presently, the Office of Economic Opportunity supports Operation Open City in New York and Metro Denver Fair Housing Center, and the Ford Foundation is underwriting seven metropolitan fair housing programs through National Urban League's "Operation Equality."

b. Government financial support for real estate brokers who take affirmative steps, often at substantial risk to themselves, to promote racial integration. Such brokers should be given contracts by HUD or the Department of Defense to provide housing consultation services for servicemen and for veterans returning to civilian life.

c. Distribution by HUD to a wide range of interested groups and individuals, of brochures describing how to achieve racial integration in local communities. The experiences of significant demonstration efforts such as Hepzibah, the National Committee on Tithing in Investment, and the programs of various stabilization groups like Crenshaw Neighbors would be relied upon. Their experiences should be used to help other groups facing similar problems.

9. Roundtables, etc.

We recommend that HUD:

a. Convene, at least annually, national and regional round-table discussions among builders, developers, mortgage bankers, real estate brokers, pension fund advisers and similar persons who have outstanding records of fostering racial integration in housing. These "knights of the roundtable" would advise HUD concerning integration strategies and could exchange ideas on the subject of integration.

b. Use as consultants to other housing professionals those housing entrepreneurs who have developed integrated housing.

c. Assist formation of non-profit technical assistance groups which would aid local groups to renew their neighborhoods on an integrated basis.

d. Aggressively publicize its housing programs for low and moderate income families at real estate industry conferences.

e. Convene a national conference of stabilization groups to discuss methods to achieve successful neighborhood stabilization and assist in establishing a National Association of Open Neighborhoods. (Just as the SEC encouraged establishment of the National Association of Securities Dealers.)

f. Sponsor free programs to train housing personnel in methods of racially integrating housing developments and of maintaining such integration.

Notes

1. See "The Impact of Housing Patterns on Job Opportunities" (National Committee Against Discrimination in Housing, 1968).
2. (Harper & Brothers, New York, 1955), p. 229.
3. *Forbidden Neighbors*, p. 230; *How the Federal Government Builds Ghettos* (National Committee Against Discrimination in Housing, 1967), p. 18.
4. Published in 1967, at 14–29.
5. The Administration program, set forth in the President's February 22, 1968, message to Congress, calls for construction on the average for the

next 10 years of 600,000 units nationwide for low and moderate income persons (with additional units made available through rehabilitation and leasing). The National Housing Conference in its 1968 resolutions recommends an annual goal of construction and rehabilitation of 1 million units for low and moderate income persons. If either of these goals is met, and a substantial fraction of the units is made available in all-white areas (by law on an open occupancy basis), substantial racial integration would occur.

6. "To Ensure Domestic Tranquility," *Reader's Digest,* May, 1968, pp. 56–57. Morris Milgram, in testimony before the National Commission on Urban Problems, also strongly supported the concept of open New Towns.

7. Senate 3029, 90th Congress, 2d session.

8. Merely to keep the inner-city non-white population at present levels would require that close to half a million non-whites would have to move from the city to the suburbs each year. Over 100,000 housing units yearly would have to be provided to house this number of people.

9. The Report of the Legislative Commission on Low Income Housing (Illinois) recommends that local housing authorities be replaced by regional housing authorities, with regions to be established by the State Housing Board, so as to "minimize untoward pressures and increase the possibility of an objective, rational and well-planned approach to public housing in local communities and throughout the State." ("For Better Housing in Illinois," 1967), pp. 41–42.

10. In the proposed Housing and Urban Development Act of 1968, a maximum of 20% of the dwelling units in any development receiving a 1% mortgage loan under the interest subsidy program could be tenanted by persons receiving rent supplements.

Acknowledgments

The basic sources for this book were my own experiences as a developer of integrated housing, my reading of the literature covering this field, and the data I assembled on racial issues in housing. These sources were supplemented by scores of interviews with builders, housing developers and managers, real-estate brokers, apartment-house owners, and residents, conducted by myself and Jack Tatum, who served as a part-time research assistant for one year. Additional research was undertaken by Donna and Dennis McDowell. Among those who provided editorial assistance, I owe a great deal to Michael Meyers (now assistant to Roy Wilkins, executive director of the NAACP), who was graciously loaned to me for an entire summer by Dr. Kenneth B. Clark, president of the Metropolitan Applied Research Center, where Michael Meyers then worked.

The greatest contribution to the book in the form of research, editing, and countless other ways, came from Gabriele Gutkind, editor of the eight-volume *International History of City Development,* and since 1973 my executive assistant. Most of the credit for having transformed a very rough manuscript into its final well-ordered shape belongs to her. She performed this exacting and vital task with patience and ability. She was also a wise and patient counselor, even when pressure of work made me a difficult colleague from time to time. When we eliminated some sections of the manuscript that she had worked on so hard with me, she accepted these cuts in good spirit as a means of strengthening the book.

I am also indebted in many different ways to the staff, boards, and advisory committees of the Milgram–Farmer group of integrated housing enterprises, in particular to James Farmer, chairman of our major companies; Gilbert Gold, president of New Hope

Housing, Inc., our chief real-estate executive; Charles N. Mason, Jr., general partner, together with me, of Partners in Housing; Hans Peters, founder and honorary co-chairman of Jop Opportunity in Skill Training, Inc. (JOIST); Joseph Hairston, past president of National Neighbors; Congressman Donald M. Fraser of Minnesota, founder, with me, and a chairman from 1964 to 1973 of SOHI, formerly National Committee on Tithing in Investment; John Michener, past president of National Neighbors and president of Sponsors of Open Housing Investment (SOHI); Jean Milgram, founder and executive director of National Neighbors, 1969–1976; and Caroline Isard and Margaret F. Aronson, Philadelphia and Washington area directors of Fund for an OPEN Society (OPEN). All were involved in countless sessions which led to many of the policies and ideas expressed in this book.

Good Neighborhood would never have been written without the encouragement and aid of the noted housing economist Louis Winnick, and his able assistant Robert W. Chandler at the Ford Foundation whose generous grant to the Metropolitan Applied Research Center (MARC), the sponsors of my work, made the book possible. Their constructive comments and critical suggestions were greatly appreciated.

Encouragement and assistance in many gentle and persistent ways was also extended by MARC's staff, led by president Dr. Kenneth B. Clark and senior vice-president Dr. Hylan G. Lewis, as well as by Jeannette Hopkins, director of their Urban Affairs Publication Program, and her successor, Mary Strong. In planning the book, they were assisted by a distinguished advisory panel, chaired by G. Franklin Edwards, chairman, department of sociology, Howard University. Serving on the panel were George and Eunice Grier, authors of *Privately Developed Interracial Housing;* Karl Taeuber, chairman, department of sociology, University of Wisconsin; and Raymond Mack, director, Center for Urban Affairs, Northwestern University. They in turn were aided by Eleanor Farrar, vice-president, MARC, Washington; Susan Gamer, associate editor, MARC Publications; Joyce Marshall, secretary, MARC Publications; and Gilbert Gold of my staff.

I was also fortunate to be able to draw upon the expertise of a number of people in the housing industry who gave generously of their time and spoke frankly about one of the most delicate problems faced by the industry: will those who plan, build, sell, and finance housing finally grant minorities the opportunity to live where they please? Some of these people, in particular mortgage banker Ferd Kramer; Harry Madway, life member of the board of directors of the National Association of Home Builders; and Leon Weiner, past president of the same organization and president of the National Housing Conference, deserve my grateful acknowledgment.

Many kindnesses were shown to me by black and white realtors (members of the National Association of Realtors) and realtists (members of the predominantly black National Association of Real Estate Brokers). Foremost among these were Joseph Battle, realtor and past president of National Neighbors; Frederick D. Gaines, member of the Pennsylvania Real Estate Commission; and I. Maximilian Martin, president of Berean Savings Association, the nation's oldest minority-managed insured savings bank. Discussions with white brokers were often off the record because of their still frequent admission that, despite fair housing laws, they would not show housing to minorities in white areas.

The preparation of the manuscript took a number of years. It was written while continuing my work as a developer of integrated housing. The information gained from the research and interviews gave me fresh insights into new techniques to strengthen integrated neighborhoods and open closed areas. The use of incentive mortgages for pro-integration housing moves as practiced by Fund for an OPEN Society (OPEN), a nonprofit mortgage fund which James Farmer and I founded in 1975, grew out of the studies for this book.

I would never have ventured into the field of developing integrated housing without the encouragement of builder William M. Smelo and, after his death, of his widow Anna Smelo, and his daughter Grace, my first wife. Supported by their wisdom and patience, I learned how to be a housing developer and set out on a course I have not deviated from. Mrs. Smelo and Grace (the latter now a distinguished housing economist) understood the housing industry, its pitfalls, and its great potential for bringing about changes that will one day raze the walls of segregation. Our shared conviction that multiracial housing can become a reality, helped me launch my first integrated developments. Their attorney, my friend Fred Creamer, also encouraged my efforts with confidence and advice.

Others, especially A. Philip Randolph, labor leader, and Pauli Murray, poet and lawyer, have influenced my thoughts and actions more than I can say. So did my wife Lorna, whose critical suggestions during the final stages of revising the manuscript were invaluable. I am also deeply grateful to my four sisters—Ida, Miriam, Esther, and Mary—who gave me the vision of social democracy and guided my path to the "Deerfield Station" and far beyond.

Among those (now deceased) who greatly assisted my work were Irving J. Fain, Eliot D. Pratt, Chester Carlson, Eleanor Roosevelt, Kivie Kaplan, Max Weinrib, Patrick Crowley, Judge William H. Hastie, Jr., and my brother Jack Milgram. With the exception of the last five, they served on the board of my first national company, Modern Community Developers, later known as Planned Communities. Each made a unique contribution to my integrated housing companies by investing not only their funds but also their knowledge and leadership.

October, 1976

Morris Milgram
Greenbelt Knoll
Philadelphia

Organizations and Corporations Mentioned in the Text

American Baptist Home Mission Society
(now Board of National Ministries)
Valley Forge, Pennsylvania 19481

American Baptist Service Corporation
Valley Forge, Pennsylvania 19481

American Friends Service Committee
1501 Cherry Street
Philadelphia, Pennsylvania 19102

Baltimore Neighborhoods, Inc.
32 West 25th Street
Baltimore, Maryland 21218

Berean Savings Association
5228 Chestnut Street
Philadelphia, Pennsylvania 19139

Blue Hills Civic Association
61 Euclid Street West
Hartford, Connecticut 06112

ORGANIZATIONS AND CORPORATIONS

Cedar-Riverside Associates, Inc.
1929 South Fifth Street
Minneapolis, Minnesota 55404

Columbia Association
Columbia, Maryland 21043

Connecticut Housing Investment Fund, Inc.
121 Tremont Street
Hartford, Connecticut 06105

Cooperative Assistance Fund
2021 K Street, NW
Washington, D.C. 20006

Crenshaw Neighbors
4034 Buckingham Road, Apt. 214
Los Angeles, California 90008

Draper & Kramer
30 West Monroe Street
Chicago, Illinois 60603

Fair Housing Contact Service
Humanity House
475 West Market Street
Akron, Ohio 44303

Foundation for Cooperative Housing
1001 15th Street, NW
Washington, D.C. 20005

Friends Neighborhood Guild
703 North 8th Street
Philadelphia, Pennsylvania 19123

ORGANIZATIONS AND CORPORATIONS

Fund for an OPEN Society
9803 Roosevelt Blvd.
Philadelphia, Pennsylvania 19114

Glenwood Lake Neighborhood Association
38 Lakeside Drive
New Rochelle, New York 10801

Greater Dallas Housing Opportunity Center, Inc.
426 Wilson Building
Dallas, Texas 75201

Gulf Reston, Inc.
11440 Isaac Newton Square, North
Reston, Virginia 22090

Home Investments Fund
116 South Michigan Avenue
Chicago, Illinois 60603

Housing Opportunities Made Equal (HOME)
1490 Jefferson Avenue
Buffalo, New York 14208

Housing Opportunities Made Equal (HOME)
503 East Main Street
Richmond, Virginia 23219

Hyde Park-Kenwood Community Conference
1400 East 53rd Street
Chicago, Illinois 60615

Leadership Council for Metropolitan Open Communities
407 South Dearborn Street
Chicago, Illinois 60605

ORGANIZATIONS AND CORPORATIONS

Miami Valley Regional Planning Commission
Dayco Building
333 West First Street
Dayton, Ohio 45402

Mid-Peninsula Coalition Housing Fund
430 Sherman Avenue
Palo Alto, California 94306

Mutual Ownership Development Foundation
795 Turk
San Francisco, California 94102

Mutual Real Estate Investment Trust (M-REIT)
41 East 42nd Street
New York, New York 10017

National Association of Home Builders
15th and M Streets, NW
Washington, D.C. 20005

National Committee Against Discrimination in Housing
1425 H Street, NW
Washington, D.C. 20005

National Corporation for Housing Partnerships
1133 15th Street, NW
Washington, D.C. 20005

National Council of the Churches of Christ in the U.S.A.
475 Riverside Drive
New York, New York 10027

National Housing Partnership
1133 15th Street, NW
Washington, D.C. 20005

ORGANIZATIONS AND CORPORATIONS

National Neighbors
17 Maplewood Mall
Philadelphia, Pennsylvania 19144

Nineteenth Ward Community Association
541 Thurston Road
Rochester, New York 14619

Northeast Community Organization
5662 The Alameda
Baltimore, Maryland 21239

Operation Equality
4102 Lee Road
Cleveland, Ohio 44128

Organization for a Better Austin
5641 West Chicago Avenue
Chicago, Illinois 60651

Real Estate Research Corporation (Anthony Downs)
72 West Adams Street
Chicago, Illinois 60603

Shaker Communities
3494 Lee Road
Suite 207
Shaker Heights, Ohio 44120

Sponsors of Open Housing Investment (SOHI)
1914 Connecticut Avenue, NW
Washington, D.C. 20009

Suburban Action Institute
257 Park Avenue South
New York, New York 10010

ORGANIZATIONS AND CORPORATIONS

Techni Co-op, Inc.
1010 Washington Blvd.
Stamford, Connecticut 06901

Unitarian Universalist Association
25 Beacon Street
Boston, Massachusetts 02108

United Housing Foundation
465 Grand
New York, New York 10002

University City Home Rental Trust
515 West Point Avenue
St. Louis, Missouri 63130

Washington Center for Metropolitan Studies
1717 Massachusetts Avenue, NW
Washington, D.C. 20036

Westchester Residential Opportunities, Inc.
470 Mamaroneck Avenue
White Plains, New York 10605

Windsor Hill Association
% Charles Cluxton
7202 Lawina Road
Baltimore, Maryland 21216

Index

INDEX